Sola Scriptura

Topical Bible Study Series

Module 1

Robert Coleridge

Dedication

I dedicate this book first and foremost to Jesus Christ, the "main thing," who alone provides the only way to Heaven through His sacrifice at Calvary, offering the free gift of salvation to all who accept it. I am deeply grateful to my wife, Terry, who patiently endures my daily question, "What does the Bible say about that?" To my parents, siblings, and children, thank you for the invaluable lessons you've taught me about living out the faith. I also want to thank my fellow believers in Christ who gently corrected me when I was wrong and helped me grow in truth and love. I'm especially appreciative of my brothers and sisters in Christ at our local church who continually help me keep the main thing, the main thing—thank you, Jeff, for that reminder. I'm thankful for the godly pastors, professors, and preachers from whom I've learned so much over the years. A special thanks goes to Pastor Schad and his wonderful wife, Lisa, of NCF, for faithfully following the leading of God the Holy Spirit for the glory of God the Father, under the lordship of God the Son. Each of you has played a meaningful role in shaping this journey, and I thank God for you all.

TABLE OF CONTENTS

Preface

In an age of moral confusion and shifting truths, the unchanging authority of God's Word stands as a beacon for those who seek clarity, purpose, and hope. *Sola Scriptura*—"Scripture Alone"—is more than a doctrine; it is a call to return to the source of truth, to let the Bible shape not only our beliefs, but our daily lives.

This volume marks the first module of a multi-part series designed to explore the Christian life through the lens of Scripture. Each module is carefully curated to build upon the last, offering readers a deeper understanding of faith, doctrine, and practical living. In this installment—Module 1: we begin by examining what it means to walk with Christ, live by the Spirit, and embrace our identity as God's people.

With over 60 topical studies, this book covers foundational themes such as the Word of God, discipleship, holiness, stewardship, community, spiritual growth, and prayer. Each topic includes key Scriptures, sound teaching, personal reflection questions, and life applications making it ideal for personal devotions, group studies, or sermon preparation.

Future modules will be released as separate volumes, diving deeper into topics such as doctrinal discernment, spiritual warfare, emotional healing, cultural engagement, and the hope of eternity. Together, these modules will provide a comprehensive discipleship path rooted entirely in the Bible useful for individual studies or group studies. I have found in group studies that having each person do the study before meeting and then discussing their responses, reactions, and applications to be very helpful.

My hope is that this work inspires you not just to study Scripture, but to live it. May it awaken a deeper hunger for God's truth, ignite transformation, and equip you to stand firm in faith with grace and conviction.

For the glory of God alone,

Robert Coleridge
May 2025

Sola Scriptura 1:1
The Word of God

FOCUS: EXPLORING THE POWER, AUTHORITY, AND PURPOSE OF GOD'S WORD IN GUIDING AND TRANSFORMING LIVES.

PRIMARY SCRIPTURE:

- Psalm 119:9-16
- Hebrews 4:12
- 2 Timothy 3:16-17

ADDITIONAL SCRIPTURE:

- Joshua 1:8
- Romans 15:4
- James 1:22-25

BIBLICAL TEACHING:

- Scripture is God-breathed, authoritative, and profitable for teaching, rebuking, and equipping believers (2 Timothy 3:16-17).
- The Word of God is alive and active, cutting through to the heart of human thoughts and intentions (Hebrews 4:12).
- Meditating on and obeying Scripture leads to spiritual success and growth (Joshua 1:8, Psalm 119:11).

QUESTIONS AND ANSWERS:

1. **How has God's Word guided or transformed your life?**

   - It provides wisdom, direction, and comfort (Psalm 119:105, Romans 15:4). Personal transformation occurs when the Word is applied (James 1:22).

2. **What does it mean for Scripture to be "living and active"?**

   - Scripture is dynamic, relevant to every generation, and penetrates to convict, encourage, and transform (Hebrews 4:12).

3. **How can you ensure the Bible remains central to your daily decisions?**

   - Regular reading, meditation, and prayer for application ensure its guidance (Psalm 1:2-3).

APPLICATIONS:

1. Dedicate time daily to study and meditate on Scripture.

2. Memorize one verse this week that applies to a current challenge.

PRAYER PROMPTS:

1. Thank God for His Word and its life-changing power.

2. Ask for understanding and application of Scripture in your life.

Sola Scriptura 1:2

Our Identity in Christ

FOCUS: UNDERSTANDING WHO WE ARE IN CHRIST AND LIVING IN THE FREEDOM OF OUR REDEEMED IDENTITY.

PRIMARY SCRIPTURE:

- Galatians 2:20
- Colossians 3:1-4
- Ephesians 1:3-14

ADDITIONAL SCRIPTURE:

- 2 Corinthians 5:17
- Romans 8:1-2
- John 1:12-13

BIBLICAL TEACHING:

- Believers are new creations in Christ, no longer condemned (2 Corinthians 5:17, Romans 8:1).
- Our identity is rooted in being chosen, redeemed, and adopted by God through Jesus (Ephesians 1:4-5).
- Setting our minds on heavenly things aligns us with our eternal destiny (Colossians 3:1-4).

QUESTIONS AND ANSWERS:

1. **How does understanding your identity in Christ affect your self-worth?**

   - It reminds us that our value comes from God's love and redemption, not from achievements (Romans 5:8, John 3:16).

2. **What does it mean to set your mind on things above?**

   - To focus on eternal truths and live with heaven's priorities (Colossians 3:2).

3. **How can you reflect your identity in Christ to others?**

   - By showing love, humility, and integrity in all relationships (Matthew 5:16, 1 Peter 2:9).

APPLICATIONS:

1. Write down truths about your identity in Christ and review them daily.

2. Share your testimony with someone this week.

PRAYER PROMPTS:

1. Thank God for your new identity in Christ.

2. Pray for strength to reflect Christ in all areas of your life.

Sola Scriptura 1:3

The Holiness of God

FOCUS: RECOGNIZING GOD'S ABSOLUTE HOLINESS AND ITS IMPLICATIONS FOR WORSHIP AND LIVING.

PRIMARY SCRIPTURE:

- Isaiah 6:1-8
- 1 Peter 1:15-16
- Revelation 4:8-11

ADDITIONAL SCRIPTURE:

- Exodus 15:11
- Leviticus 19:2
- Hebrews 12:14

BIBLICAL TEACHING:

- God's holiness is His unique purity and moral perfection (Isaiah 6:3).
- Believers are called to reflect God's holiness in their conduct (1 Peter 1:15-16).
- Worship in heaven centers on God's holiness and majesty (Revelation 4:8-11).

QUESTIONS AND ANSWERS:

1. **What does Isaiah's vision of God's holiness teach us about humility?**
   - It reveals human sinfulness and the need for cleansing by God (Isaiah 6:5-7).

2. **How does God's holiness challenge the way you approach sin and grace?**

   - It shows the seriousness of sin and the incredible gift of grace through Christ (Romans 6:23).

3. **In what areas of your life is God calling you to reflect His holiness?**

   - In speech, actions, and relationships, striving for purity and integrity (Colossians 3:12-14).

APPLICATIONS:

1. Identify one area where you need to pursue holiness this week.

2. Spend time in worship, meditating on God's holiness.

PRAYER PROMPTS:

1. Praise God for His holiness and perfection.

2. Ask for strength to reflect His holiness in your life.

Sola Scriptura 1:4

The Cost of Discipleship

FOCUS: EMBRACING THE SACRIFICES AND REWARDS OF FOLLOWING JESUS WHOLEHEARTEDLY.

PRIMARY SCRIPTURE:

- Luke 9:23-26
- Philippians 3:7-11
- Matthew 16:24-25

ADDITIONAL SCRIPTURE:

- Mark 10:29-30
- Romans 12:1
- Matthew 10:37-39

BIBLICAL TEACHING:

- Discipleship requires denying self, taking up the cross, and prioritizing Christ above all (Luke 9:23).
- The rewards of knowing Christ far outweigh earthly sacrifices (Philippians 3:7-8).
- True freedom and purpose are found in surrendering to Jesus (Matthew 16:25).

QUESTIONS AND ANSWERS:

1. **What does "denying yourself" look like in your daily life?**
   - It means surrendering personal desires for God's will (Luke 22:42).

2. **How does following Jesus challenge cultural ideas of success?**

    • True success is measured by faithfulness to God, not by wealth or status (Mark 10:43-45).

3. **How does this teaching help you find true freedom and purpose in Christ?**

    • It liberates from sin and aligns life with God's eternal plan (John 8:36, Matthew 11:28-30).

APPLICATIONS:

1. Identify one area where you can surrender more fully to Christ.

2. Reflect on past sacrifices for Christ and how He has blessed them.

PRAYER PROMPTS:

1. Thank God for the privilege of following Jesus.

2. Pray for strength to remain faithful, even when it costs you.

Sola Scriptura 1:5

Walking in the Spirit

FOCUS: LIVING IN STEP WITH THE HOLY SPIRIT'S GUIDANCE AND EXPERIENCING HIS POWER IN DAILY LIFE.

PRIMARY SCRIPTURE:

- Galatians 5:16-26
- Romans 8:9-17
- John 14:26

ADDITIONAL SCRIPTURE:

- Ephesians 5:18
- Acts 1:8
- 2 Timothy 1:7

BIBLICAL TEACHING:

- Walking in the Spirit involves relying on His guidance to resist sinful desires and produce spiritual fruit (Galatians 5:16-23).
- The Spirit empowers believers to live victoriously and confirms their identity as God's children (Romans 8:14-17).
- The Holy Spirit teaches, reminds, and strengthens believers for their daily walk (John 14:26).

QUESTIONS AND ANSWERS:

1. **How does walking by the Spirit transform your daily decisions?**

   - The Spirit convicts, guides, and empowers choices that align with God's will (John 16:13, Galatians 5:16).

2. **Which fruit of the Spirit do you find most challenging to cultivate, and why?**

   - Answers will vary but may include patience or self-control. Cultivation requires reliance on the Spirit (Galatians 5:22-23).

3. **How can you become more sensitive to the Spirit's guidance?**

   - Spend time in prayer, study Scripture, and respond promptly to His prompting (1 Thessalonians 5:19).

APPLICATIONS:

1. Choose one fruit of the Spirit to intentionally develop this week.
2. Spend time in prayer asking for the Spirit's guidance in a specific area.

PRAYER PROMPTS:

1. Praise God for the gift of the Holy Spirit.
2. Ask for the Spirit's power to live victoriously over sin.

Sola Scriptura 1:6

Stewardship and Generosity

FOCUS: HONORING GOD WITH OUR TIME, TALENTS, AND RESOURCES, AND REFLECTING HIS GENEROSITY IN OUR LIVES.

PRIMARY SCRIPTURE:

- 2 Corinthians 9:6-8
- Matthew 25:14-30
- Proverbs 3:9-10

ADDITIONAL SCRIPTURE:

- Malachi 3:10
- 1 Timothy 6:17-19
- Acts 20:35

BIBLICAL TEACHING:

- Stewardship involves managing God-given resources for His glory (Proverbs 3:9-10).
- Generosity reflects God's character and results in blessings for the giver and receiver (2 Corinthians 9:6-8).
- Faithful stewardship of talents and resources brings eternal rewards (Matthew 25:14-30).

QUESTIONS AND ANSWERS:

1. **What does it mean to honor God with your time, talents, and resources?**

- It means recognizing that all we have is from God and using it to serve Him and others (Psalm 24:1, Colossians 3:23).

2. **How does trusting God's provision free you to be generous?**

   - Trusting God eliminates fear of lack, allowing believers to give freely (Philippians 4:19).

3. **In what ways can you use your resources to bless others and glorify God?**

   - Through tithing, supporting missions, and meeting the needs of others (Proverbs 19:17).

APPLICATIONS:

1. Identify one way you can practice generosity this week.

2. Reflect on how you can better steward your time or talents for God's glory.

PRAYER PROMPTS:

1. Thank God for His provision and ask for wisdom to be a faithful steward.

2. Pray for opportunities to demonstrate generosity.

Sola Scriptura 1:7

Rest and Sabbath

FOCUS: EMBRACING THE GIFT OF REST AS PART OF GOD'S DESIGN AND TRUSTING IN HIS PROVISION.

PRIMARY SCRIPTURE:

- Exodus 20:8-11
- Matthew 11:28-30
- Hebrews 4:9-11

ADDITIONAL SCRIPTURE:

- Genesis 2:2-3
- Isaiah 58:13-14
- Mark 2:27-28

BIBLICAL TEACHING:

- Sabbath rest is a divine command and a gift that renews our relationship with God (Exodus 20:8-11).
- Jesus invites the weary to find spiritual rest in Him (Matthew 11:28-30).
- True Sabbath rest points to the eternal rest we have in Christ (Hebrews 4:9-11).

QUESTIONS AND ANSWERS:

1. **How does keeping the Sabbath honor God's design for rest?**
   - It acknowledges God's provision and sets aside time to worship Him (Genesis 2:3, Exodus 20:11).

2. **How can Sabbath rest restore your relationship with God?**

   - It provides time to reflect, pray, and realign priorities with God's will (Psalm 23:1-3).

3. **What practical steps can you take to incorporate rhythms of rest into your life?**

   - Schedule regular times for rest and minimize distractions (Mark 6:31).

APPLICATIONS:

1. Set aside a day this week to intentionally rest and reconnect with God.

2. Identify distractions that prevent you from embracing rest and eliminate them.

PRAYER PROMPTS:

1. Praise God for creating rest and ask for discipline to embrace it.

2. Pray for peace and renewal in your relationship with God.

Sola Scriptura 1:8

Suffering and Sovereignty

FOCUS: TRUSTING GOD'S SOVEREIGNTY AND PURPOSE IN THE MIDST OF TRIALS AND SUFFERING.

PRIMARY SCRIPTURE:

- Romans 8:28-39
- Job 1:21-22
- 2 Corinthians 4:16-18

ADDITIONAL SCRIPTURE:

- James 1:2-4
- 1 Peter 4:12-13
- 2 Corinthians 1:3-4

BIBLICAL TEACHING:

- God works all things for good for those who love Him and are called according to His purpose (Romans 8:28).
- Suffering refines faith and produces perseverance (James 1:2-4).
- God's sovereignty assures us that even in trials, His plans are perfect (Job 1:21, 2 Corinthians 4:17-18).

QUESTIONS AND ANSWERS:

1. **How does God's sovereignty give you hope in times of suffering?**
   - It reassures us that nothing is outside of God's control and He has a purpose in every trial (Isaiah 46:9-10).

15

2. **What lessons has God taught you through past trials?**

   - Personal answers may include reliance on God's strength, deepened faith, or renewed priorities (2 Corinthians 12:9-10).

3. **How does focusing on eternal glory change your perspective on pain?**

   - It shifts focus from temporary struggles to the joy and restoration that await believers in eternity (Revelation 21:4).

APPLICATIONS:

   1. Reflect on a trial you've faced and write down how God used it for good.

   2. Share a testimony of God's faithfulness during suffering with someone this week.

PRAYER PROMPTS:

   1. Thank God for His presence and sovereignty in your trials.

   2. Pray for endurance and trust during current difficulties.

Sola Scriptura 1:9

Spiritual Warfare

FOCUS: EQUIPPING OURSELVES WITH THE ARMOR OF GOD TO STAND AGAINST SPIRITUAL OPPOSITION.

PRIMARY SCRIPTURE:

- Ephesians 6:10-18
- 2 Corinthians 10:3-5
- James 4:7

ADDITIONAL SCRIPTURE:

- 1 Peter 5:8-9
- Colossians 2:15
- Matthew 4:1-11

BIBLICAL TEACHING:

- Believers are engaged in a spiritual battle and must rely on God's strength and protection (Ephesians 6:10-11).
- The armor of God equips us to resist the enemy and stand firm in faith (Ephesians 6:12-17).
- Prayer is a vital weapon in spiritual warfare (Ephesians 6:18, James 4:7).

QUESTIONS AND ANSWERS:

1. **How does each piece of the armor of God equip you for spiritual battles?**

   - The belt of truth counters lies, the shield of faith extinguishes doubt, and the sword of the Spirit combats with God's Word (Ephesians 6:14-17).

2. **What steps can you take to guard your thoughts and align them with Scripture?**

   - Meditate on God's Word (Psalm 119:11), take thoughts captive (2 Corinthians 10:5), and reject lies (Philippians 4:8).

3. **How does prayer strengthen your ability to resist the devil?**

   - Prayer connects believers to God's power and provides wisdom and protection (Philippians 4:6-7).

APPLICATIONS:

1. Pray through the armor of God daily, asking for protection and strength.

2. Identify an area of your life where spiritual battles are most evident and commit it to prayer.

PRAYER PROMPTS:

1. Thank God for providing spiritual armor to stand against the enemy.

2. Ask for discernment and strength in spiritual warfare.

Sola Scriptura 1:10

The Mission of the Church

FOCUS: UNDERSTANDING THE CHURCH'S ROLE IN SPREADING THE GOSPEL AND MAKING DISCIPLES.

PRIMARY SCRIPTURE:

- Matthew 28:18-20
- Acts 1:8
- Ephesians 4:11-16

ADDITIONAL SCRIPTURE:

- Romans 10:14-15
- 1 Peter 3:15
- John 20:21

BIBLICAL TEACHING:

- The Great Commission calls all believers to make disciples of all nations (Matthew 28:18-20).
- The Holy Spirit empowers the Church for witness and mission (Acts 1:8).
- God equips His Church with spiritual gifts to build His kingdom (Ephesians 4:11-12).

QUESTIONS AND ANSWERS:

1. **How does the Great Commission apply to your personal life?**
   - Every believer is called to share the gospel and disciple others (2 Corinthians 5:20).

2. **What role does the Church play in building God's kingdom?**

   - The Church serves as God's witness, nurturing believers and proclaiming Christ to the world (1 Peter 2:9).

3. **How can you actively support your local church's mission and outreach efforts?**

   - Through prayer, giving, volunteering, and evangelism (Hebrews 10:24-25).

APPLICATIONS:

1. Share the gospel with someone in your circle this week.

2. Volunteer in a ministry or outreach initiative at your church.

PRAYER PROMPTS:

1. Pray for your church's leaders and outreach efforts.

2. Ask for boldness and opportunities to share your faith.

Sola Scriptura 1:11

Eternal Perspective

FOCUS: LIVING WITH ETERNITY IN MIND AND TRUSTING IN GOD'S PROMISES FOR THE FUTURE.

PRIMARY SCRIPTURE:

- 2 Corinthians 4:16-18
- Revelation 21:1-5
- Romans 8:18-25

ADDITIONAL SCRIPTURE:

- Philippians 3:20-21
- John 14:1-3
- 2 Peter 3:13

BIBLICAL TEACHING:

- Eternal hope sustains believers through temporary challenges (2 Corinthians 4:17-18).
- Heaven is a place of restoration, where God dwells with His people (Revelation 21:3-4).
- Living with eternity in mind shapes priorities and decisions (Philippians 3:20-21).

QUESTIONS AND ANSWERS:

1. **How does focusing on eternity change the way you handle current challenges?**

   - It provides hope and perspective, knowing trials are temporary (Romans 8:18).

2. **What excites you most about the new heaven and new earth?**

   - The absence of pain and sin, and the joy of eternal communion with God (Revelation 21:4).

3. **How can you live today with eternity in mind?**

   - By prioritizing God's kingdom, serving others, and investing in eternal values (Matthew 6:33).

APPLICATIONS:

1. Identify one area where you can prioritize eternal values over temporary concerns.

2. Meditate on Revelation 21:1-5 and journal your thoughts on God's promises.

PRAYER PROMPTS:

1. Thank God for the hope of eternity and His promises.

2. Pray for an eternal perspective in your decisions and relationships.

Sola Scriptura 1:12

Soul Annihilation vs. Soul Eternity

FOCUS: EXPLORING THE BIBLICAL TEACHING OF THE ETERNAL NATURE OF THE SOUL AND REFUTING THE CONCEPT OF SOUL ANNIHILATION.

PRIMARY SCRIPTURE:

- Matthew 25:46
- Daniel 12:2
- Revelation 20:10-15

ADDITIONAL SCRIPTURE:

- John 5:28-29
- Ecclesiastes 12:7
- 2 Thessalonians 1:9

BIBLICAL TEACHING:

- The Bible consistently teaches that the soul exists eternally, either in eternal life or eternal punishment (Matthew 25:46).
- Both the righteous and the wicked will be resurrected for eternal destinies (John 5:28-29).
- Hell is a place of ongoing conscious torment, not annihilation (Revelation 20:10, Revelation 14:11).

QUESTIONS AND ANSWERS:

1. **What do passages like Matthew 25:46 teach about the eternal nature of the soul?**

   - The use of the same word "eternal" for both life and punishment emphasizes their unending nature.

2. **How does the Bible describe the eternal destinies of the righteous and the wicked?**

   - The righteous experience eternal life with God, while the wicked face eternal separation and punishment (Daniel 12:2, Revelation 21:1-8).

3. **How does the idea of soul annihilation conflict with God's justice?**

   - Annihilation minimizes the gravity of sin and fails to reflect the infinite justice required for rebellion against an infinite God (Romans 6:23, 2 Thessalonians 1:9).

APPLICATIONS:

1. Share the gospel with someone who has questions about eternity.

2. Reflect on the weight of eternal realities in your own life.

PRAYER PROMPTS:

1. Praise God for offering eternal life through Jesus.

2. Pray for those who have not yet trusted Christ for salvation.

Sola Scriptura 1:13
Double Predestination and Its Refutation

FOCUS: UNDERSTANDING AND REFUTING THE DOCTRINE OF DOUBLE PREDESTINATION WHILE AFFIRMING GOD'S JUSTICE, SOVEREIGNTY, AND LOVE.

PRIMARY SCRIPTURE:

- Romans 8:29-30
- 1 Timothy 2:3-4
- 2 Peter 3:9

ADDITIONAL SCRIPTURE:

- John 3:16
- Ezekiel 18:23
- Romans 9:22-24

BIBLICAL TEACHING:

- Predestination in Scripture focuses on God's foreknowledge and plan for salvation (Romans 8:29).
- God desires all to be saved and provides the means for salvation through Christ (1 Timothy 2:4, John 3:16).
- Romans 9 highlights God's sovereignty but does not teach that He predestines some to damnation.

QUESTIONS AND ANSWERS:

1. **What does the Bible teach about predestination and God's foreknowledge?**

   - God's foreknowledge allows Him to predestine believers to conform to Christ's image without overriding free will (Ephesians 1:4-5).

2. **How does the concept of double predestination conflict with God's character?**

   - It contradicts Scriptures that affirm God's love for all and His desire for repentance (Ezekiel 18:23, 2 Peter 3:9).

3. **How should believers respond to the doctrine of predestination in faith and evangelism?**

   - Trust God's plan and actively share the gospel, knowing His desire is for all to be saved (2 Corinthians 5:20).

APPLICATIONS:

1. Reflect on God's sovereignty and mercy, and trust His plan for your life.

2. Share God's love and the hope of salvation with someone this week.

PRAYER PROMPTS:

1. Thank God for His mercy and justice.

2. Pray for clarity and humility in understanding His purposes.

Sola Scriptura 1:14

The Reality of Hell

FOCUS: UNDERSTANDING THE BIBLICAL TEACHING ON HELL AS A PLACE OF ETERNAL SEPARATION FROM GOD, ITS IMPLICATIONS, AND ITS PURPOSE.

PRIMARY SCRIPTURE:

- Matthew 25:41-46
- Revelation 20:10-15
- Luke 16:19-31

ADDITIONAL SCRIPTURE:

- Mark 9:43-48
- 2 Thessalonians 1:8-9
- John 3:16-18

BIBLICAL TEACHING:

- Hell is a place of eternal punishment for sin, prepared for the devil and his angels (Matthew 25:41).
- The wicked face eternal separation from God and conscious torment (Revelation 20:10-15).
- God's justice requires that sin be judged, and hell demonstrates the seriousness of rejecting His grace (Romans 6:23).

QUESTIONS AND ANSWERS:

1. **What does the Bible teach about the nature and purpose of hell?**

   - Hell is a just punishment for sin and eternal separation from God's presence (2 Thessalonians 1:9).

2. **How do passages like Matthew 25:41 describe the eternal nature of hell?**

   - Hell is described as "eternal fire," signifying unending judgment for those who reject God.

3. **How does the reality of hell motivate believers to share the gospel?**

   - It instills urgency to share the good news so others can avoid eternal separation (Romans 10:14-15).

APPLICATIONS:

1. Reflect on the seriousness of rejecting God's grace and renew your commitment to evangelism.
2. Pray for the salvation of specific individuals.

PRAYER PROMPTS:

1. Thank God for His justice and mercy.
2. Pray for compassion and urgency in sharing the gospel.

Sola Scriptura 1:15

Church Discipline

FOCUS: UNDERSTANDING THE BIBLICAL PRINCIPLES AND PURPOSE OF CHURCH DISCIPLINE AS A MEANS OF RESTORATION, PROTECTION, AND HOLINESS.

PRIMARY SCRIPTURE:

- Matthew 18:15-17
- 1 Corinthians 5:1-5
- Galatians 6:1

ADDITIONAL SCRIPTURE:

- Hebrews 12:6
- 2 Thessalonians 3:14-15
- James 5:19-20

BIBLICAL TEACHING:

- Church discipline aims to restore the sinner, protect the church, and honor God's holiness (Galatians 6:1).
- The process involves private correction, group intervention, and church involvement when necessary (Matthew 18:15-17).
- Discipline reflects God's love and desire for repentance (Hebrews 12:6).

QUESTIONS AND ANSWERS:

1. **What is the purpose of church discipline according to Scripture?**
   - To restore the sinner to fellowship with God and the church, and to protect the church's witness (1 Corinthians 5:6-7).

2. **How does Matthew 18:15-17 outline the process of addressing sin within the church?**

   - Private correction, small group intervention, and, if necessary, church involvement with the goal of restoration.

3. **Why is gentleness and restoration essential in church discipline?**

   - It ensures discipline reflects God's grace and love, aiming for repentance and healing (Galatians 6:1).

APPLICATIONS:

1. Encourage accountability and honesty in your church relationships.

2. Support church leaders as they navigate difficult disciplinary situations.

PRAYER PROMPTS:

1. Pray for wisdom and grace in addressing sin within the church.

2. Thank God for His loving discipline that brings restoration.

Sola Scriptura 1:16
Personal Responsibility with Regards to Salvation

FOCUS: UNDERSTANDING OUR ROLE IN RESPONDING TO GOD'S GIFT OF SALVATION AND HOW PERSONAL RESPONSIBILITY PLAYS A PART IN FAITH, REPENTANCE, AND PERSEVERANCE.

PRIMARY SCRIPTURE:

- **Philippians 2:12-13**:
- **Romans 10:9-10**
- **Ezekiel 18:30-32**

ADDITIONAL SCRIPTURE:

- **John 3:16-18**
- **Acts 2:38**
- **James 2:17**
- **2 Corinthians 5:10**

BIBLICAL TEACHING:

- Salvation is a gift of God's grace, not earned by works (Ephesians 2:8-9), but it requires a personal response of faith, repentance, and obedience (Romans 10:9-10, Acts 2:38).

- Personal responsibility involves aligning our lives with God's will and actively pursuing spiritual growth, empowered by His grace (Philippians 2:12-13).

- God desires all people to be saved, but He holds individuals accountable for their response to His offer of salvation (Ezekiel 18:30-32, 2 Corinthians 5:10).

QUESTIONS AND ANSWERS:

1. **What is our personal responsibility in responding to God's gift of salvation?**

   - We must respond in faith (trusting in Jesus), repentance (turning from sin), and obedience (living a life aligned with God's Word) (Romans 10:9-10, Acts 2:38).

2. **How do Philippians 2:12-13 and Ephesians 2:8-9 complement each other?**

   - Salvation is entirely a work of God's grace (Ephesians 2:8-9), but Philippians 2:12-13 teaches that we are to actively "work out" our salvation by applying it in daily life, knowing God empowers us to do so.

3. **Why is repentance a necessary part of salvation?**

   - Repentance reflects a genuine turning away from sin and a decision to follow Christ, which aligns with God's call for holiness (Ezekiel 18:30, Luke 13:3).

4. **How does personal responsibility shape our daily walk with God?**

   - It leads to intentional practices like prayer, Scripture study, and obedience, fostering spiritual growth and alignment with God's will (2 Timothy 2:15).

5. **What role does accountability play in salvation?**

   - Each person is accountable for their response to God's offer of salvation and their choices, which reflect their faith (2 Corinthians 5:10, James 2:17).

APPLICATIONS:

1. **Self-Reflection**: Take time this week to reflect on your personal response to God's call. Have you truly placed your faith in Him, repented, and obeyed His Word?

2. **Take Action**: Identify one area where you can align your life more closely with God's will—whether in relationships, habits, or spiritual disciplines.

PRAYER PROMPTS:

1. **Confession**: Ask God to reveal areas in your life where you need to take greater responsibility for your faith.

2. **Commitment**: Commit to daily living out your salvation through faith, repentance, and obedience.

3. **Intercession**: Pray for friends or family members who have not yet responded to God's gift of salvation.

Sola Scriptura 1:17

The Role of Prayer in the Believer's Life

FOCUS: UNDERSTANDING THE IMPORTANCE OF PRAYER AS A MEANS OF COMMUNICATION WITH GOD, ALIGNING OUR WILL WITH HIS, AND EXPERIENCING HIS POWER IN OUR LIVES.

PRIMARY SCRIPTURE:

- Philippians 4:6-7
- Matthew 6:9-13
- James 5:16

ADDITIONAL SCRIPTURE:

- 1 Thessalonians 5:16-18
- Romans 8:26-27
- Ephesians 6:18
- Mark 11:24

BIBLICAL TEACHING:

- Prayer is a vital connection to God, expressing dependence, gratitude, and faith (Philippians 4:6).

- Jesus modeled prayer as central to His relationship with the Father and taught His followers how to pray (Matthew 6:9-13).

- Prayer is powerful, effective, and a means through which God accomplishes His will (James 5:16, Ephesians 6:18).

- The Holy Spirit intercedes for us, strengthening our prayers even in our weakness (Romans 8:26).

QUESTIONS AND ANSWERS:

1. Why is prayer essential in the life of a believer?

- Prayer is how we communicate with God, seek His will, and experience His peace (Philippians 4:6-7). It's also a means of accessing His power and aligning with His purposes (James 5:16, Mark 11:24).

2. What can we learn from the Lord's Prayer in Matthew 6:9-13?

- The Lord's Prayer teaches us to honor God's name, seek His kingdom, depend on Him for daily needs, and forgive others. It reflects a balance of worship, petition, and submission to God's will.

3. How does prayer impact anxiety and worry?

- Prayer replaces anxiety with God's peace, as we release our burdens to Him and trust His provision (Philippians 4:6-7).

4. What role does faith play in prayer?

- Faith is essential for effective prayer. Believing that God hears and answers according to His will brings confidence (Mark 11:24, James 1:6).

5. How can the Holy Spirit help us in our prayer life?

- The Spirit intercedes for us when we don't know how to pray, aligning our prayers with God's will (Romans 8:26-27).

APPLICATIONS:

1. **Develop a Prayer Routine**: Set aside intentional time daily for prayer, incorporating elements of praise, confession, thanksgiving, and supplication.

2. **Pray for Others**: Identify specific people or situations to pray for, and commit to lifting them up regularly.

3. **Keep a Prayer Journal**: Record your prayers and reflect on how God answers over time.

PRAYER PROMPTS:

1. **Adoration**: Praise God for His greatness, love, and faithfulness.

2. **Confession**: Ask for forgiveness in areas where you've failed to depend on Him in prayer.

3. **Intercession**: Pray for the needs of others, your church, and global concerns.

4. **Petition**: Bring your own concerns and desires to God, trusting in His perfect will.

Sola Scriptura 1:18
The Fruit of the Spirit and Spiritual Growth

FOCUS: UNDERSTANDING THE FRUIT OF THE SPIRIT AS EVIDENCE OF A LIFE TRANSFORMED BY CHRIST AND HOW BELIEVERS GROW SPIRITUALLY THROUGH THE SPIRIT'S WORK.

PRIMARY SCRIPTURE:

- Galatians 5:22-23
- John 15:4-5
- 2 Peter 1:5-8

ADDITIONAL SCRIPTURE:

- Matthew 7:16-20
- Philippians 1:9-11
- Colossians 1:10
- Romans 8:6-9

BIBLICAL TEACHING:

- The Fruit of the Spirit is the outward evidence of the Holy Spirit's transformative work in the believer's life (Galatians 5:22-23).

- Spiritual growth comes through abiding in Christ, as we are nourished by His Word and empowered by the Spirit (John 15:4-5).

- God calls believers to continually grow in Christlike qualities, reflecting His character to the world (2 Peter 1:5-8).

- Bearing fruit glorifies God and testifies to the authenticity of our faith (Matthew 7:16, Colossians 1:10).

QUESTIONS AND ANSWERS:

1. **What does it mean to bear the Fruit of the Spirit?**

   - Bearing fruit means exhibiting qualities such as love, joy, and peace, which reflect Christ's character and result from living by the Spirit (Galatians 5:22-23, John 15:4-5).

2. **How can we abide in Christ to grow spiritually?**

   - Abiding in Christ involves staying connected to Him through prayer, Scripture, and obedience. Spiritual growth occurs as His Word and Spirit shape us (John 15:4, 2 Timothy 3:16).

3. **What is the relationship between the Fruit of the Spirit and spiritual maturity?**

   - The Fruit of the Spirit is evidence of spiritual maturity, demonstrating growth in Christlike character and dependence on the Spirit (2 Peter 1:5-8, Philippians 1:9-11).

4. **How do we identify areas where spiritual growth is needed?**

   - Self-examination through prayer, Scripture, and accountability can reveal areas where Christ's character is not fully evident (Psalm 139:23-24, Matthew 7:16).

5. **How can believers cultivate the Fruit of the Spirit in their lives?**

   - By surrendering to the Spirit's guidance, practicing spiritual disciplines, and seeking opportunities to apply Christlike qualities in daily interactions (Romans 8:6-9, Colossians 3:12-14).

APPLICATIONS:

1. **Reflect on the Fruit**: Identify one area of the Fruit of the Spirit where growth is needed (e.g., patience, kindness) and focus on cultivating it through prayer and intentional practice.

2. **Remain in Christ**: Commit to spending daily time in God's Word and prayer to deepen your connection to Him.

3. **Seek Accountability**: Invite a trusted friend or mentor to encourage and challenge you in your spiritual growth.

PRAYER PROMPTS:

1. **Confession**: Ask God to forgive areas where the Fruit of the Spirit is lacking in your life.

2. **Supplication**: Pray for the Spirit's work in producing fruit that reflects Christ's character.

3. **Intercession**: Pray for your church community to grow in spiritual maturity and unity.

Sola Scriptura 1:19

Faith and Works

FOCUS: EXPLORING THE RELATIONSHIP BETWEEN FAITH AND WORKS, UNDERSTANDING SALVATION BY GRACE, AND HOW GOOD WORKS REFLECT GENUINE FAITH.

PRIMARY SCRIPTURE:

- Ephesians 2:8-10
- James 2:14-26
- Matthew 5:16

ADDITIONAL SCRIPTURE:

- Titus 3:4-8
- Galatians 5:6
- John 15:8
- Philippians 2:12-13

BIBLICAL TEACHING:

- Salvation is a gift of grace received through faith, not earned by works (Ephesians 2:8-9).

- Genuine faith is evidenced by good works, which are the natural outcome of a transformed life (James 2:17, Matthew 7:20).

- Works glorify God and demonstrate His love to others, advancing His kingdom on earth (Matthew 5:16, Titus 3:8).

QUESTIONS AND ANSWERS:

1. **What is the relationship between faith and works?**

   o Faith is the foundation of salvation, and works are its evidence, showing the fruit of a genuine relationship with God (James 2:18, John 15:8).

2. **How do Ephesians 2:8-10 and James 2:14-26 complement each other?**

   • Ephesians emphasizes salvation as God's gift, while James highlights the visible proof of faith through actions. Together, they show that works flow naturally from saving faith.

3. **What is the danger of relying on works for salvation?**

   • It denies God's grace and makes salvation a matter of human effort, which Scripture clearly rejects (Romans 3:20, Galatians 2:16).

4. **How can works glorify God and point others to Him?**

   • Good works reflect God's character, draw others to Christ, and demonstrate His love in tangible ways (Matthew 5:16, 1 Peter 2:12).

5. **What steps can you take to align your faith with action?**

   • Actively serve others, seek opportunities to love in deed, and ask God to reveal ways to live out your faith daily (Galatians 5:13-14).

APPLICATIONS:

1. **Identify a Need**: Look for a specific way to serve others this week, whether in your church, community, or workplace.

2. **Examine Your Faith**: Reflect on whether your works align with your professed faith and take steps to act accordingly.

PRAYER PROMPTS:

1. Thank God for saving you by grace through faith.

2. Ask for opportunities to demonstrate your faith through good works.

3. Pray for a heart that glorifies God through loving service to others.

Sola Scriptura 1:20

Christian Community

FOCUS: UNDERSTANDING THE IMPORTANCE OF FELLOWSHIP, UNITY, AND ACCOUNTABILITY IN THE BODY OF CHRIST.

PRIMARY SCRIPTURE:

- Acts 2:42-47
- Hebrews 10:24-25
- 1 Corinthians 12:12-27

ADDITIONAL SCRIPTURE:

- Galatians 6:2
- Colossians 3:12-15
- Proverbs 27:17
- John 13:34-35

BIBLICAL TEACHING:

- Christian community is essential for spiritual growth, mutual encouragement, and bearing one another's burdens (Acts 2:42, Galatians 6:2).

- Every believer has a role in the Body of Christ, contributing to its unity and function (1 Corinthians 12:12-27).

- Fellowship demonstrates Christ's love to the world and strengthens believers in their walk (John 13:34-35, Hebrews 10:24-25).

QUESTIONS AND ANSWERS:

1. **Why is Christian community essential for spiritual growth?**
   - It provides encouragement, accountability, and opportunities to serve and grow together (Hebrews 10:24-25, Proverbs 27:17).

2. **What does Acts 2:42-47 teach about fellowship?**
   - Fellowship involves shared teaching, prayer, generosity, and worship, fostering unity and spiritual growth.

3. **How does the metaphor of the body in 1 Corinthians 12 apply to the Church?**
   - Each member has a unique role, and all are necessary for the body to function properly, emphasizing unity and diversity.

4. **What challenges can arise in Christian community, and how can they be resolved?**
   - Challenges like conflict or misunderstanding can be resolved through forgiveness, humility, and love (Colossians 3:13, Ephesians 4:3).

5. **How can you contribute to strengthening your Christian community?**
   - By serving, praying for others, and fostering an atmosphere of love and encouragement (Galatians 6:10, John 13:35).

APPLICATIONS:

1. **Engage in Fellowship**: Attend a small group or church gathering regularly to deepen connections with other believers.

2. **Serve Others**: Identify a way to meet a need within your Christian community this week.

PRAYER PROMPTS:

1. Thank God for the gift of Christian fellowship and unity in the Church.

2. Pray for the growth, strength, and unity of your local church.

3. Ask for guidance in how you can contribute to the Body of Christ.

Sola Scriptura 1:21

Perseverance in Trials

FOCUS: TRUSTING GOD'S FAITHFULNESS AND DEVELOPING ENDURANCE THROUGH LIFE'S CHALLENGES.

PRIMARY SCRIPTURE:

- James 1:2-4
- Romans 5:3-5
- Hebrews 12:1-3

ADDITIONAL SCRIPTURE:

- 2 Corinthians 4:16-18
- 1 Peter 5:10
- Matthew 11:28-30
- Isaiah 40:31

BIBLICAL TEACHING:

- Trials are a means of spiritual growth, refining faith and producing perseverance (James 1:2-3).

- God's presence and promises provide hope and strength during suffering (Romans 5:5, 2 Corinthians 4:17-18).

- Fixing our eyes on Jesus, the perfect example of endurance, helps us persevere through difficulties (Hebrews 12:1-3).

QUESTIONS AND ANSWERS:

1. **How can trials produce spiritual growth?**

   - Trials test faith, develop perseverance, and shape character, leading to maturity (James 1:2-4, Romans 5:3-4).

2. **What role does hope play in persevering through trials?**

   - Hope in God's promises sustains us, reminding us that suffering is temporary and glory eternal (Romans 8:18, 2 Corinthians 4:17).

3. **How does Hebrews 12:1-3 encourage perseverance?**

   - By focusing on Jesus, who endured the cross for the joy set before Him, believers find strength and inspiration to endure.

4. **What practical steps can help you persevere in trials?**

   - Trusting God's Word, seeking prayer and support, and remembering His faithfulness (Isaiah 40:31, Matthew 11:28).

5. **How can you encourage others who are facing trials?**

   - Through prayer, sharing Scripture, and offering practical support (Galatians 6:2, 2 Corinthians 1:3-4).

APPLICATIONS:

1. **Remember God's Faithfulness**: Write down ways God has been faithful in past trials and reflect on His promises.

2. **Encourage Someone**: Reach out to someone going through a trial and offer prayer or practical help.

PRAYER PROMPTS:

1. Praise God for His faithfulness in all circumstances.

2. Pray for strength and endurance to persevere through challenges.

3. Lift up others who are facing trials, asking God to sustain them.

Sola Scriptura 1:22

Spiritual Gifts

FOCUS: UNDERSTANDING THE ROLE OF SPIRITUAL GIFTS IN BUILDING UP THE CHURCH AND FULFILLING GOD'S PURPOSES.

PRIMARY SCRIPTURE:

- 1 Corinthians 12:4-7
- Romans 12:6-8
- Ephesians 4:11-13

ADDITIONAL SCRIPTURE:

- 1 Peter 4:10-11
- 2 Timothy 1:6-7
- 1 Corinthians 14:12

BIBLICAL TEACHING:

- Spiritual gifts are given by the Holy Spirit to every believer for the purpose of glorifying God and serving the Church (1 Corinthians 12:4-7, 1 Peter 4:10).

- Each believer has unique gifts that contribute to the unity and growth of the Body of Christ (Ephesians 4:11-13).

- God calls us to recognize, develop, and use our gifts in faith, humility, and love (Romans 12:6-8, 1 Corinthians 14:12).

QUESTIONS AND ANSWERS:

1. **What is the purpose of spiritual gifts?**

   - To glorify God, strengthen the Church, and fulfill His mission on earth (1 Corinthians 12:7, Ephesians 4:12).

2. **How can you discover your spiritual gifts?**

   - Through prayer, Scripture study, serving in various ministries, and seeking confirmation from the Body of Christ (Romans 12:6, 1 Peter 4:10).

3. **How can spiritual gifts promote unity in the Church?**

   - By recognizing that all gifts come from the same Spirit and are meant to complement one another, promoting interdependence and mutual encouragement (1 Corinthians 12:12-27).

4. **What happens when spiritual gifts are neglected or misused?**

   - Neglecting gifts limits the Church's effectiveness, while misuse can cause division or harm (1 Corinthians 14:26, 1 Peter 4:11).

5. **How can you actively use your gifts for God's glory?**

   - Seek opportunities to serve, be willing to step out in faith, and stay rooted in love and humility (Ephesians 4:15-16, Romans 12:11).

APPLICATIONS:

1. **Discover Your Gifts**: Take time to identify your spiritual gifts through prayer, Scripture, and seeking counsel from others in your community.

2. **Use Your Gifts**: Commit to serving in a ministry or activity that allows you to exercise your gifts.

3. **Encourage Others**: Affirm the gifts you see in fellow believers and encourage them to use their gifts for God's glory.

PRAYER PROMPTS:

1. Thank God for the spiritual gifts He has given you.

2. Pray for wisdom in using your gifts to serve others and glorify God.

3. Intercede for your church community to grow in unity and effectiveness through the use of spiritual gifts.

Sola Scriptura 1:23

The Power of Forgiveness

FOCUS: UNDERSTANDING GOD'S CALL TO FORGIVE OTHERS AS HE HAS FORGIVEN US AND THE FREEDOM THAT COMES FROM PRACTICING FORGIVENESS.

PRIMARY SCRIPTURE:

- Colossians 3:13
- Matthew 6:14-15
- Ephesians 4:31-32

ADDITIONAL SCRIPTURE:

- Matthew 18:21-35
- Psalm 103:10-12
- Luke 23:34

BIBLICAL TEACHING:

- Forgiveness is rooted in God's forgiveness of us through Christ (Ephesians 4:32).

- Unforgiveness hinders our relationship with God and others, while forgiveness brings freedom and restoration (Matthew 6:14-15, Hebrews 12:15).

- Forgiveness is not condoning sin but releasing the offender and entrusting justice to God (Romans 12:19).

QUESTIONS AND ANSWERS:

1. **Why is forgiveness central to the Christian life?**
   - Forgiveness reflects God's character and demonstrates the grace we have received in Christ (Colossians 3:13, Luke 23:34).

2. **What does the Parable of the Unforgiving Servant teach us about forgiveness?**
   - It shows the vastness of God's mercy and the expectation that we extend that mercy to others (Matthew 18:21-35).

3. **How does unforgiveness affect our spiritual and emotional health?**
   - It creates bitterness, disrupts relationships, and distances us from God's peace (Hebrews 12:15, Matthew 6:15).

4. **What steps can you take to forgive someone who has deeply hurt you?**
   - Pray for God's help, release the offense to Him, and choose to act in love toward the person (Matthew 5:44, Romans 12:20).

5. **How can forgiving others deepen your understanding of God's grace?**
   - It reminds us of the immense debt God forgave us and helps us experience His love more fully (Psalm 103:10-12, Ephesians 4:32).

APPLICATIONS:

1. **Examine Your Heart**: Identify any areas of unforgiveness in your life and take steps to release those offenses to God.

2. **Seek Reconciliation**: If possible, reach out to someone with whom you need to reconcile and take the first step toward forgiveness.

3. **Extend Grace**: Practice daily forgiveness in small offenses to cultivate a forgiving heart.

PRAYER PROMPTS:

1. Thank God for His forgiveness and grace in your life.

2. Ask for strength to forgive those who have wronged you.

3. Pray for healing and restoration in broken relationships.

Sola Scriptura 1:24

Living a Life of Gratitude

FOCUS: CULTIVATING A HEART OF GRATITUDE TO GOD IN ALL CIRCUMSTANCES AND EXPRESSING THAT GRATITUDE THROUGH WORDS AND ACTIONS.

PRIMARY SCRIPTURE:

- 1 Thessalonians 5:16-18
- Colossians 3:15-17
- Psalm 100:4-5

ADDITIONAL SCRIPTURE:

- Philippians 4:6-7
- Ephesians 5:19-20
- Luke 17:11-19

BIBLICAL TEACHING:

- Gratitude is the will of God for believers, fostering joy, peace, and a deeper relationship with Him (1 Thessalonians 5:16-18, Philippians 4:6-7).

- A thankful heart reflects trust in God's goodness and sovereignty, even in difficult circumstances (Colossians 3:15-17, Romans 8:28).

- Expressing gratitude glorifies God and encourages others to see His faithfulness (Psalm 100:4-5, Luke 17:18).

QUESTIONS AND ANSWERS:

1. **Why is gratitude important in the Christian life?**

   - Gratitude acknowledges God's blessings, deepens trust in Him, and cultivates joy in all circumstances (Philippians 4:6-7, 1 Thessalonians 5:18).

2. **What does the healing of the ten lepers teach us about gratitude?**

   - It highlights the importance of returning to thank God, recognizing His blessings, and glorifying Him for His goodness (Luke 17:15-19).

3. **How can you give thanks even in difficult circumstances?**

   - By trusting God's sovereignty, focusing on His past faithfulness, and finding reasons to rejoice in His goodness (Romans 8:28, Habakkuk 3:17-19).

4. **What practical ways can you cultivate gratitude in your daily life?**

   - Keep a gratitude journal, intentionally thank others, and focus on blessings instead of complaints (Ephesians 5:19-20).

5. **How does gratitude impact your relationship with God and others?**

   - It strengthens trust in God, fosters joy, and deepens connections through acts of kindness and appreciation (Colossians 3:15, Psalm 100:4).

APPLICATIONS:

1. **Start a Gratitude Journal**: Write down three things you are thankful for each day.

2. **Express Thanks**: Verbally thank someone who has impacted your life or blessed you recently.

3. **Praise God in Prayer**: Dedicate a prayer time solely to praising and thanking God for His goodness.

PRAYER PROMPTS:

1. Thank God for specific blessings in your life.
2. Praise Him for His goodness, even in challenging situations.
3. Pray for a heart that consistently recognizes and celebrates God's faithfulness.

Sola Scriptura 1:25

Evangelism

FOCUS: UNDERSTANDING THE BELIEVER'S RESPONSIBILITY TO SHARE THE GOSPEL AND PRACTICAL WAYS TO FULFILL THE GREAT COMMISSION.

PRIMARY SCRIPTURE:

- Matthew 28:19-20
- Romans 10:14-15
- Acts 1:8

ADDITIONAL SCRIPTURE:

- 1 Peter 3:15
- 2 Corinthians 5:20
- Mark 16:15

BIBLICAL TEACHING:

- Evangelism is the responsibility of every believer, commanded by Jesus in the Great Commission (Matthew 28:19-20).

- Sharing the gospel involves proclaiming the message of salvation through Christ, both in words and actions (Romans 10:14-15, 1 Peter 3:15).

- The Holy Spirit empowers believers to be effective witnesses, giving boldness and guiding their efforts (Acts 1:8).

QUESTIONS AND ANSWERS:

1. **Why is evangelism important for every believer?**

   - It fulfills Jesus' command, brings glory to God, and gives others the opportunity to receive salvation (Matthew 28:19, 2 Corinthians 5:20).

2. **What role does the Holy Spirit play in evangelism?**

   - The Spirit empowers believers, provides boldness, and opens hearts to receive the gospel (Acts 1:8, John 16:8-11).

3. **What are some practical ways to share the gospel in daily life?**

   - Engage in conversations about faith, live a Christlike example, and invite others to church or small group studies (1 Peter 3:15, Colossians 4:5-6).

4. **How can fear or hesitation in evangelism be overcome?**

   - By trusting in God's power, praying for courage, and remembering that salvation is God's work, not ours (2 Timothy 1:7, Romans 1:16).

5. **What does it mean to be an ambassador for Christ (2 Corinthians 5:20)?**

   - It means representing Jesus in the world, sharing His message, and living in a way that reflects His love and truth.

APPLICATIONS:

1. **Identify Opportunities**: Pray for and seek out specific opportunities to share the gospel this week.

2. **Prepare Your Testimony**: Write out and practice sharing your personal story of salvation in a concise way.

3. **Support Missions**: Find ways to support local or global missions through prayer, giving, or participation.

PRAYER PROMPTS:

1. Thank God for the opportunity to share the gospel and the people He's placed in your life.

2. Pray for boldness and clarity when sharing your faith.

3. Intercede for those who have yet to know Christ.

Sola Scriptura 1:26

The Second Coming of Christ

FOCUS: UNDERSTANDING THE PROMISES AND IMPLICATIONS OF CHRIST'S RETURN, AND HOW IT SHAPES THE BELIEVER'S LIFE.

PRIMARY SCRIPTURE:

- Matthew 24:30-31
- 1 Thessalonians 4:16-17
- Revelation 22:12-13

ADDITIONAL SCRIPTURE:

- Acts 1:11
- 2 Peter 3:10-13
- Titus 2:13

BIBLICAL TEACHING:

- The Second Coming of Christ is a core Christian hope, when Jesus will return to judge the world, reward believers, and establish His eternal kingdom (Matthew 24:30-31, 2 Timothy 4:8).

- Believers are called to live in readiness, anticipating His return with faith and holiness (Titus 2:13, 1 Thessalonians 5:2-6).

- Christ's return motivates evangelism, perseverance in trials, and a focus on eternal priorities (2 Peter 3:10-12, Revelation 22:12).

QUESTIONS AND ANSWERS:

1. **What does Scripture teach about the manner of Christ's return?**

   - Jesus will return visibly, powerfully, and gloriously to gather His people and judge the world (Acts 1:11, Matthew 24:30).

2. **Why is the Second Coming referred to as the "blessed hope"?**

   - It assures believers of Christ's ultimate victory over sin and death and the fulfillment of His promises (Titus 2:13, Revelation 21:3-4).

3. **How should believers prepare for Christ's return?**

   - By living holy and godly lives, staying alert, and fulfilling His mission (2 Peter 3:11, 1 Thessalonians 5:6).

4. **What are the signs of Christ's return described in Scripture?**

   - Widespread moral decay, natural disasters, persecution, and the spread of the gospel to all nations (Matthew 24:4-14).

5. **How does the promise of Christ's return impact daily life?**

   - It inspires hope, motivates evangelism, and encourages perseverance in trials (2 Corinthians 4:17-18, Revelation 22:12).

APPLICATIONS:

1. **Evaluate Priorities**: Reflect on whether your life reflects readiness for Christ's return, and adjust as needed.

2. **Share the Hope**: Encourage someone who is struggling by reminding them of the promise of Christ's return.

3. **Pray for Readiness**: Ask God to help you live faithfully in anticipation of Jesus' return.

PRAYER PROMPTS:

1. Thank God for the promise of Christ's return and the hope it brings.

2. Pray for perseverance and faithfulness as you wait for His coming.

3. Intercede for those who do not yet know Jesus, that they may come to faith before His return.

Sola Scriptura 1:27

Heaven

FOCUS: UNDERSTANDING THE BIBLICAL DESCRIPTION OF HEAVEN, THE HOPE IT PROVIDES, AND HOW IT SHAPES OUR LIVES TODAY.

PRIMARY SCRIPTURE:

- Revelation 21:1-4
- John 14:1-3
- Philippians 3:20-21

ADDITIONAL SCRIPTURE:

- 2 Corinthians 5:8
- Isaiah 65:17
- Matthew 6:19-21
- Hebrews 13:14

BIBLICAL TEACHING:

- Heaven is a place of eternal fellowship with God, where believers experience perfect joy, peace, and freedom from suffering (Revelation 21:4).

- Jesus promised to prepare a place for His followers, affirming the reality and certainty of heaven (John 14:2-3).

- Heaven is the believer's true home, motivating us to live with eternal priorities (Philippians 3:20, Hebrews 13:14).

QUESTIONS AND ANSWERS:

1. **What does Scripture reveal about the nature of heaven?**

   - Heaven is where God dwells with His people, free from pain, death, and sin (Revelation 21:3-4, Isaiah 65:17).

2. **How does Jesus' promise in John 14:1-3 provide hope?**

   - It assures believers that Jesus is preparing a personal place for them and will return to bring them into His presence.

3. **What does it mean to store treasures in heaven (Matthew 6:19-21)?**

   - It means investing in eternal things, like faith, love, and service, rather than temporary material possessions.

4. **How does knowing your citizenship is in heaven shape your daily life?**

   - It encourages detachment from worldly values and a focus on living for God's kingdom (Philippians 3:20, Colossians 3:2).

5. **What are you most looking forward to about heaven?**

   - Answers may include being in God's presence, reuniting with loved ones, or experiencing perfect peace and joy.

APPLICATIONS:

1. **Reflect on Eternity**: Take time to meditate on the promises of heaven and how they bring hope in your current circumstances.

2. **Live for Eternity**: Identify one way you can prioritize eternal values over worldly concerns this week.

3. **Encourage Others**: Share the hope of heaven with someone who is struggling or grieving.

PRAYER PROMPTS:

1. Thank God for the promise of heaven and the hope it provides.
2. Praise Him for the assurance of eternal life through Christ.
3. Pray for opportunities to share the hope of heaven with others.

Sola Scriptura 1:28

Judgment

FOCUS: UNDERSTANDING GOD'S RIGHTEOUS JUDGMENT AND ITS IMPLICATIONS FOR BELIEVERS AND UNBELIEVERS.

PRIMARY SCRIPTURE:

- 2 Corinthians 5:10
- Revelation 20:11-15
- Romans 14:10-12

ADDITIONAL SCRIPTURE:

- Matthew 25:31-46
- John 5:28-29
- Ecclesiastes 12:14
- Hebrews 9:27

BIBLICAL TEACHING:

- God's judgment is righteous, impartial, and based on His perfect knowledge of every person (Romans 2:6, Ecclesiastes 12:14).

- Believers will stand before the judgment seat of Christ to receive rewards for their faithfulness (2 Corinthians 5:10).

- Unbelievers will face the great white throne judgment, where rejection of Christ results in eternal separation from God (Revelation 20:11-15).

QUESTIONS AND ANSWERS:

1. **What is the difference between the judgment seat of Christ and the great white throne judgment?**

   - The judgment seat of Christ is for believers, focusing on rewards for faithful service. The great white throne judgment is for unbelievers, determining eternal separation from God (2 Corinthians 5:10, Revelation 20:15).

2. **Why is God's judgment necessary?**

   - It upholds God's justice and holiness, bringing accountability for sin and vindicating righteousness (Romans 2:5, Ecclesiastes 12:14).

3. **How should believers prepare for the judgment seat of Christ?**

   - By living faithfully, serving others, and investing in God's kingdom (Matthew 6:20, 1 Corinthians 3:13-14).

4. **How does the reality of judgment motivate evangelism?**

   - It creates urgency to share the gospel, knowing that unbelievers face eternal separation without Christ (John 3:18, Romans 10:14-15).

5. **What does it mean to give an account of yourself to God (Romans 14:12)?**

   - It means acknowledging how you have used your life, time, and resources in service to Him and others.

APPLICATIONS:

1. **Examine Your Life**: Reflect on how you are living in light of God's coming judgment and make necessary adjustments.

2. **Share the Gospel**: Reach out to someone who needs to hear about Jesus and the hope of salvation.

3. **Live Faithfully**: Commit to using your time, talents, and resources for God's glory.

PRAYER PROMPTS:

1. Praise God for His justice and holiness.
2. Thank Him for the assurance of salvation through Christ.
3. Pray for boldness to share the gospel with urgency.

Sola Scriptura 1:29

Sanctification

FOCUS: UNDERSTANDING SANCTIFICATION AS THE PROCESS OF BECOMING MORE LIKE CHRIST THROUGH THE WORK OF THE HOLY SPIRIT.

PRIMARY SCRIPTURE:

- 1 Thessalonians 4:3-4
- Romans 12:1-2
- Philippians 1:6

ADDITIONAL SCRIPTURE:

- Hebrews 10:14
- 2 Corinthians 3:18
- Galatians 5:16-25

BIBLICAL TEACHING:

- Sanctification is the process by which believers are made holy, set apart for God's purposes, and conformed to Christ's image (Romans 12:1-2, 2 Corinthians 3:18).

- It is both God's work and the believer's responsibility, as we cooperate with the Holy Spirit through obedience and faith (Philippians 2:12-13).

- Sanctification begins at salvation and continues throughout the believer's life until glorification (Hebrews 10:14, Philippians 1:6).

QUESTIONS AND ANSWERS:

1. **What is the difference between justification and sanctification?**

    *   Justification is a one-time act of being declared righteous before God through faith in Christ. Sanctification is the ongoing process of growing in holiness (Romans 5:1, 1 Thessalonians 4:3).

2. **How does the Holy Spirit contribute to sanctification?**

    *   The Spirit transforms believers, produces spiritual fruit, and empowers obedience (Galatians 5:16-18, 2 Corinthians 3:18).

3. **What role do believers play in sanctification?**

    *   By yielding to the Spirit, practicing spiritual disciplines, and avoiding sin, believers cooperate with God's work (Romans 12:1-2, Philippians 2:12-13).

4. **How can trials contribute to sanctification?**

    *   Trials refine faith, develop perseverance, and deepen dependence on God (James 1:2-4, 1 Peter 1:6-7).

5. **What evidence shows progress in sanctification?**

    *   Increased Christlikeness, growth in the Fruit of the Spirit, and greater victory over sin (Galatians 5:22-23, Romans 6:14).

APPLICATIONS:

1. **Assess Your Walk**: Identify one area where God is calling you to grow in holiness and take practical steps to change.

2. **Walk by the Spirit**: Commit to daily surrender and obedience to the Holy Spirit.

3. **Seek Accountability**: Partner with a mentor or small group to encourage spiritual growth.

PRAYER PROMPTS:

1. Thank God for His transforming work in your life.

2. Ask for strength and wisdom to cooperate with the Spirit in your sanctification.

3. Pray for perseverance in the process of becoming more like Christ.

Sola Scriptura 1:30

The Trinity

FOCUS: UNDERSTANDING THE BIBLICAL FOUNDATION OF THE TRINITY AND ITS SIGNIFICANCE IN OUR RELATIONSHIP WITH GOD.

PRIMARY SCRIPTURE:

- Matthew 28:19
- John 14:16-17
- 2 Corinthians 13:14

ADDITIONAL SCRIPTURE:

- Genesis 1:26
- Deuteronomy 6:4
- John 1:1-3
- Acts 5:3-4

BIBLICAL TEACHING:

- The Trinity is the doctrine that God is one in essence and three in persons: Father, Son, and Holy Spirit (Matthew 28:19, Deuteronomy 6:4).

- Each person of the Trinity is fully God, equal in power, yet distinct in role (John 1:1-3, Acts 5:3-4).

- The Trinity demonstrates perfect unity and relationship, reflecting God's nature and providing a model for human relationships (John 14:16-17, 2 Corinthians 13:14).

QUESTIONS AND ANSWERS:

1. **What does it mean for God to be "one in essence and three in persons"?**

   - God is one being but exists eternally as Father, Son, and Spirit, each fully divine and distinct in personhood (Matthew 28:19, John 1:1).

2. **How do the roles of the Trinity interact in salvation?**

   - The Father initiates salvation, the Son accomplishes it through His death and resurrection, and the Spirit applies it by regenerating and indwelling believers (Ephesians 1:3-14, John 14:16).

3. **Why is understanding the Trinity important for believers?**

   - It deepens our worship, helps us understand God's relational nature, and strengthens our understanding of Scripture (2 Corinthians 13:14, John 14:26).

4. **What practical impact does the Trinity have on daily life?**

   - It reminds us of God's presence (Spirit), love (Father), and sacrifice (Son), encouraging worship, relationship, and mission (Romans 8:15-17).

5. **How can we explain the Trinity to others?**

   - Use clear Scripture references and analogies cautiously, emphasizing God's mystery and revealed truth (Matthew 28:19, John 1:1).

APPLICATIONS:

1. **Meditate on the Trinity**: Reflect on how each person of the Trinity has impacted your life.

2. **Deepen Worship**: Incorporate worship and prayer to the Father, Son, and Spirit.

3. **Teach Others**: Share a clear explanation of the Trinity with someone who has questions.

PRAYER PROMPTS:

1. Praise the Father for His creation and love.
2. Thank the Son for His sacrifice and salvation.
3. Ask the Spirit for guidance and strength in your daily walk.

Sola Scriptura 1:31

The Beatitudes

FOCUS: UNDERSTANDING THE BEATITUDES AS A DESCRIPTION OF KINGDOM LIVING AND HOW THEY SHAPE THE BELIEVER'S CHARACTER.

PRIMARY SCRIPTURE:

- Matthew 5:1-12
- Luke 6:20-23

ADDITIONAL SCRIPTURE:

- Isaiah 61:1-3
- Psalm 34:18
- Romans 12:14-21

BIBLICAL TEACHING:

- The Beatitudes reveal the heart and character of those who belong to God's kingdom, emphasizing humility, mercy, righteousness, and peace (Matthew 5:3-12).

- They contrast worldly values, calling believers to depend on God and prioritize eternal rewards (Luke 6:20-23).

- Living out the Beatitudes reflects Christ's character and blesses others (Romans 12:14-21).

QUESTIONS AND ANSWERS:

1. **What does it mean to be "poor in spirit" (Matthew 5:3)?**

   - It means recognizing one's spiritual neediness and dependence on God's grace (Psalm 34:18, Isaiah 66:2).

2. **How can mourning lead to blessing (Matthew 5:4)?**

   - Mourning over sin and brokenness invites God's comfort and healing (2 Corinthians 7:10, Isaiah 61:1-3).

3. **Why are the meek blessed (Matthew 5:5)?**

   - Meekness reflects humility and submission to God, leading to inheritance of His promises (Psalm 37:11, Matthew 11:29).

4. **How do peacemakers reflect God's character (Matthew 5:9)?**

   - They mirror God's reconciling work in Christ, promoting harmony and reconciliation (2 Corinthians 5:18-20, Romans 12:18).

5. **What does it mean to be persecuted for righteousness (Matthew 5:10-12)?**

   - It means facing opposition for living according to God's truth, with the assurance of eternal reward (John 15:18-20, 2 Timothy 3:12).

APPLICATIONS:

1. **Live Out a Beatitude**: Choose one Beatitude to intentionally practice this week.

2. **Reflect on Character**: Evaluate how your life reflects kingdom values and make adjustments.

3. **Encourage Others**: Share how living the Beatitudes has impacted your life.

PRAYER PROMPTS:

1. Thank God for the blessings of His kingdom.
2. Ask for strength to embody the values of the Beatitudes.
3. Pray for those who are persecuted for their faith.

Sola Scriptura 1:32

Overcoming Sin

FOCUS: UNDERSTANDING GOD'S PROVISION FOR VICTORY OVER SIN AND HOW BELIEVERS CAN LIVE IN FREEDOM AND OBEDIENCE.

PRIMARY SCRIPTURE:

- Romans 6:12-14
- 1 Corinthians 10:13
- Galatians 5:16

ADDITIONAL SCRIPTURE:

- 1 John 1:9
- Hebrews 12:1-2
- Psalm 119:9-11

BIBLICAL TEACHING:

- Christ's death and resurrection provide freedom from sin's power, enabling believers to live in righteousness (Romans 6:11-14).

- God is faithful to provide strength and a way of escape in temptation (1 Corinthians 10:13).

- Walking by the Spirit and abiding in Christ equips believers to overcome sin and grow in holiness (Galatians 5:16, John 15:5).

QUESTIONS AND ANSWERS:

1. **What does it mean to not let sin reign in your body (Romans 6:12)?**

   - It means resisting sin's control and choosing obedience to God instead (Romans 6:19, Colossians 3:5).

2. **How does God provide help in temptation (1 Corinthians 10:13)?**

   - He limits temptation, provides strength, and shows a way out, enabling believers to endure.

3. **What role does the Holy Spirit play in overcoming sin (Galatians 5:16)?**

   - The Spirit empowers believers to resist sinful desires and produce godly fruit (Romans 8:13, Galatians 5:22-23).

4. **How can Scripture help in overcoming sin?**

   - Memorizing and meditating on God's Word equips believers with truth to resist temptation (Psalm 119:11, Matthew 4:4).

5. **What should you do when you fall into sin?**

   - Confess it to God, repent, and trust in His forgiveness and cleansing (1 John 1:9, Proverbs 28:13).

APPLICATIONS:

1. **Identify a Struggle**: Pinpoint an area of sin in your life and seek accountability and prayer.

2. **Use God's Word**: Memorize a Scripture that addresses your struggle.

3. **Walk by the Spirit**: Commit to daily surrender and reliance on the Holy Spirit.

PRAYER PROMPTS:

1. Confess areas of sin and ask for God's forgiveness and strength.
2. Thank God for His provision of victory through Christ and the Spirit.
3. Pray for a heart that seeks holiness and resists temptation.

Sola Scriptura 1:33

Hope in Hardship

FOCUS: UNDERSTANDING THE SOURCE OF HOPE IN DIFFICULT TIMES AND HOW BELIEVERS CAN ENDURE TRIALS WITH CONFIDENCE IN GOD'S PROMISES.

PRIMARY SCRIPTURE:

- Romans 8:18
- 2 Corinthians 4:16-18
- Hebrews 6:19

ADDITIONAL SCRIPTURE:

- James 1:2-4
- Isaiah 40:31
- Psalm 34:17-18
- 1 Peter 1:6-7

BIBLICAL TEACHING:

- Hope in hardship is rooted in the promises of God, who works all things for the good of those who love Him (Romans 8:28).

- Trials are temporary and purposeful, refining faith and building character (James 1:2-4, 1 Peter 1:7).

- The hope of eternal glory gives believers strength to endure and remain faithful in suffering (2 Corinthians 4:17-18, Hebrews 6:19).

QUESTIONS AND ANSWERS:

1. **How does Romans 8:18 shape our perspective on suffering?**

   - It reminds us that our present pain is temporary and incomparable to the eternal joy awaiting us.

2. **What role does hope play in enduring hardship?**

   - Hope anchors our souls, keeping us steady and focused on God's faithfulness and promises (Hebrews 6:19).

3. **How can trials be an opportunity for growth (James 1:2-4)?**

   - Trials test and strengthen faith, producing perseverance and spiritual maturity.

4. **What practical steps can you take to maintain hope during difficult times?**

   - Pray, meditate on Scripture, surround yourself with supportive community, and focus on eternal truths (Psalm 34:18, Isaiah 40:31).

5. **How can sharing your hope encourage others?**

   - Testimonies of hope in hardship inspire others to trust God and persevere through their own trials (1 Peter 3:15).

APPLICATIONS:

1. **Cling to God's Promises**: Memorize a verse about hope to meditate on during difficulties.

2. **Encourage Someone**: Share your story of hope in hardship with someone who is struggling.

RENEW YOUR FOCUS: SPEND TIME IN PRAYER, ASKING GOD TO HELP YOU FOCUS ON HIS ETERNAL PROMISES.

PRAYER PROMPTS:

1. Thank God for being an anchor of hope in all circumstances.

2. Pray for strength and perseverance during trials.

3. Intercede for someone who is experiencing hardship, asking God to fill them with hope.

Sola Scriptura 1:34

God's Providence

FOCUS: TRUSTING IN GOD'S SOVEREIGN CONTROL AND HIS ABILITY TO BRING GOOD FROM ALL CIRCUMSTANCES.

PRIMARY SCRIPTURE:

- Romans 8:28
- Proverbs 16:9
- Genesis 50:20

ADDITIONAL SCRIPTURE:

- Psalm 139:16
- Matthew 6:26-30
- Isaiah 46:9-10
- Philippians 1:6

BIBLICAL TEACHING:

- God's providence assures believers that He is in control of all things, working out His purposes for His glory and our good (Romans 8:28, Isaiah 46:9-10).

- Even in suffering, God's providence brings redemption and growth, as seen in Joseph's story (Genesis 50:20).

- Trusting in God's providence frees believers from anxiety and encourages dependence on Him (Matthew 6:26-30, Proverbs 3:5-6).

QUESTIONS AND ANSWERS:

1. **What is God's providence, and how does it differ from fate?**

   - Providence is God's intentional, loving control over all creation, while fate implies impersonal determinism.

2. **How does Romans 8:28 bring comfort in difficult situations?**

   - It assures believers that God is using every circumstance, even hardship, for their ultimate good and His glory.

3. **How did Joseph's story demonstrate God's providence (Genesis 50:20)?**

   - God used Joseph's suffering to save many lives, showing His ability to bring good from evil.

4. **What steps can you take to trust God's providence in your life?**

   - Surrender plans to Him, reflect on past faithfulness, and rely on His Word for guidance (Proverbs 3:5-6, Philippians 4:6-7).

5. **How can understanding God's providence affect your daily decisions?**

   - It fosters humility, peace, and confidence in God's perfect plan, even when outcomes are uncertain.

APPLICATIONS:

1. **Reflect on God's Faithfulness**: Write down examples of how God has worked in your life, even in unexpected ways.

2. **Surrender Plans**: Commit a specific area of uncertainty or worry to God's care.

3. **Trust His Timing**: Meditate on Scripture passages about God's sovereignty.

PRAYER PROMPTS:

1. Praise God for His perfect plan and care in every detail of life.
2. Thank Him for working all things for your good and His glory.
3. Pray for trust and peace in situations where His providence is hard to see.

Sola Scriptura 1:35

Faithfulness in Service

FOCUS: EMBRACING THE CALL TO SERVE GOD AND OTHERS WITH PERSEVERANCE, HUMILITY, AND JOY.

PRIMARY SCRIPTURE:

- Matthew 25:21
- Colossians 3:23-24
- 1 Corinthians 15:58

ADDITIONAL SCRIPTURE:

- Philippians 2:3-4
- Galatians 6:9-10
- Hebrews 6:10
- Romans 12:11

BIBLICAL TEACHING:

- Faithfulness in service reflects a heart devoted to God, prioritizing His glory and the good of others (Colossians 3:23, Philippians 2:3-4).

- Serving with perseverance and humility honors God and blesses others, even in unseen or challenging tasks (Galatians 6:9-10, Hebrews 6:10).

- God values and rewards faithful service, calling believers to live with eternal purpose (Matthew 25:21, 1 Corinthians 15:58).

QUESTIONS AND ANSWERS:

1. **What does it mean to serve faithfully (Matthew 25:21)?**

    - It means being dependable, diligent, and joyful in fulfilling God's calling, regardless of recognition or results.

2. **How can Colossians 3:23-24 shape your approach to work and service?**

    - It reminds us that all tasks are ultimately for God, motivating excellence and integrity.

3. **What are practical ways to serve others with humility (Philippians 2:3-4)?**

    - By putting others' needs first, avoiding pride, and offering help in small or unseen ways.

4. **What encouragement does Galatians 6:9 provide when service feels tiring?**

    - It assures us that perseverance in doing good will result in a harvest of blessings in due time.

5. **How does God reward faithfulness in service (Hebrews 6:10)?**

    - God remembers every act of love and service, rewarding it both in this life and eternity.

APPLICATIONS:

1. **Serve Intentionally**: Identify a specific way you can serve in your church or community this week.

2. **Persevere in Service**: Reflect on a task where you've grown weary and recommit it to God.

3. **Encourage Fellow Servants**: Reach out to someone serving faithfully and affirm their work.

PRAYER PROMPTS:

1. Thank God for opportunities to serve Him and others.

2. Pray for strength, humility, and perseverance in service.

3. Ask for wisdom to prioritize service that aligns with God's will.

Sola Scriptura 1:36

Wisdom in Decision-Making

FOCUS: SEEKING GOD'S WISDOM AND GUIDANCE IN MAKING CHOICES THAT ALIGN WITH HIS WILL.

PRIMARY SCRIPTURE:

- Proverbs 3:5-6
- James 1:5
- Psalm 32:8

ADDITIONAL SCRIPTURE:

- Colossians 3:17
- Philippians 4:6-7
- Isaiah 30:21
- Ecclesiastes 12:13

BIBLICAL TEACHING:

- Wisdom begins with trusting God and seeking His direction through Scripture, prayer, and counsel (Proverbs 3:5-6, Psalm 32:8).

- God generously gives wisdom to those who ask in faith (James 1:5), and His peace guards the heart when decisions align with His will (Philippians 4:6-7).

- Wise decision-making reflects a heart devoted to God's purposes, considering eternal priorities over temporary concerns (Colossians 3:17, Ecclesiastes 12:13).

QUESTIONS AND ANSWERS:

1. **How does Proverbs 3:5-6 guide decision-making?**

   - It encourages complete trust in God's guidance, not relying solely on personal understanding, and promises His direction.

2. **What does James 1:5 teach about seeking wisdom?**

   - It assures that God gives wisdom generously to those who ask in faith.

3. **How can prayer and Scripture shape wise decisions?**

   - Prayer invites God's guidance, and Scripture provides principles and clarity for choices (Philippians 4:6-7, Psalm 119:105).

4. **What role does seeking counsel play in decision-making?**

   - Wise counsel from godly mentors or friends helps confirm God's direction and prevents hasty or selfish choices (Proverbs 15:22).

5. **How do eternal values influence decisions?**

   - Decisions made with eternity in mind prioritize God's glory, relationships, and kingdom work over material or fleeting concerns (Colossians 3:2, Matthew 6:33).

APPLICATIONS:

1. **Present Your Decisions**: Bring a current decision to God in prayer, asking for wisdom and peace.

2. **Seek Counsel**: Talk to a trusted mentor or friend about a choice you are facing.

3. **Evaluate Priorities**: Reflect on how your decisions align with God's eternal purposes.

PRAYER PROMPTS:

1. Thank God for being the source of wisdom and guidance.
2. Pray for clarity and discernment in specific decisions.
3. Ask for a heart that prioritizes God's will over personal desires.

Sola Scriptura 1:37

God's Faithfulness

FOCUS: TRUSTING IN GOD'S UNCHANGING NATURE AND FAITHFULNESS TO HIS PROMISES.

PRIMARY SCRIPTURE:

- Lamentations 3:22-23
- Deuteronomy 7:9
- 2 Timothy 2:13

ADDITIONAL SCRIPTURE:

- Psalm 89:1-2:
- 1 Thessalonians 5:24
- Hebrews 10:23
- Joshua 21:45

BIBLICAL TEACHING:

- God's faithfulness is rooted in His unchanging character and His commitment to fulfill His promises (Lamentations 3:22-23, Deuteronomy 7:9).

- Even when we are unfaithful, God's faithfulness remains constant, offering assurance of His love and mercy (2 Timothy 2:13).

- Remembering God's faithfulness builds trust, perseverance, and hope in every season of life (Psalm 89:1-2, Hebrews 10:23).

QUESTIONS AND ANSWERS:

1. **How does Lamentations 3:22-23 reflect God's faithfulness?**

   - It highlights His unfailing compassion, daily renewal of mercy, and greatness in keeping His promises.

2. **What does it mean that God remains faithful when we are faithless (2 Timothy 2:13)?**

   - God's character and promises do not change, even when we falter, assuring His mercy and grace.

3. **How can remembering God's past faithfulness encourage you in present challenges?**

   - Reflecting on His fulfilled promises strengthens trust and gives confidence that He will continue to be faithful (Joshua 21:45, Psalm 89:1).

4. **What role does God's faithfulness play in holding onto hope (Hebrews 10:23)?**

   - It assures believers that their hope is secure, based not on circumstances but on God's unchanging nature.

5. **How can you declare God's faithfulness to others?**

   - By sharing testimonies of His provision, mercy, and fulfilled promises (Psalm 89:1, Revelation 12:11).

APPLICATIONS:

1. **Reflect on Faithfulness**: Write down ways God has been faithful in your life.

2. **Share a Testimony**: Tell someone about a specific time God fulfilled a promise or answered prayer.

3. **Trust in Hard Times**: Remind yourself of God's faithfulness when facing a current challenge.

PRAYER PROMPTS:

1. Praise God for His unchanging faithfulness.

2. Thank Him for specific ways He has kept His promises in your life.

3. Pray for strength to trust Him in areas where His faithfulness is hard to see.

Sola Scriptura 1:38

The Role of Worship

FOCUS: EMBRACING WORSHIP AS A LIFESTYLE OF HONORING GOD WITH OUR HEARTS, WORDS, AND ACTIONS.

PRIMARY SCRIPTURE:

- John 4:23-24
- Psalm 95:6-7
- Romans 12:1

ADDITIONAL SCRIPTURE:

- Psalm 100:1-5
- Hebrews 12:28-29
- Colossians 3:16-17
- Revelation 4:11

BIBLICAL TEACHING:

- Worship is not just singing songs but a life devoted to glorifying God in spirit, truth, and action (John 4:23-24, Romans 12:1).

- True worship flows from a heart of gratitude and awe for who God is and what He has done (Psalm 100:1-5, Hebrews 12:28-29).

- Worshiping together with the Body of Christ strengthens faith and reflects God's glory to the world (Colossians 3:16-17, Psalm 95:6).

QUESTIONS AND ANSWERS:

1. **What does it mean to worship in spirit and truth (John 4:23-24)?**

   - It means worshiping authentically, led by the Holy Spirit, and grounded in the truth of God's Word.

2. **How is worship a lifestyle (Romans 12:1)?**

   - It involves offering every part of our lives—actions, words, and attitudes—as an act of devotion to God.

3. **Why is corporate worship important?**

   - It unites believers in praising God, strengthens the Church, and magnifies God's glory collectively (Psalm 95:6, Hebrews 10:24-25).

4. **How can thanksgiving shape your worship?**

   - Gratitude focuses the heart on God's goodness and deepens reverence and joy in worship (Psalm 100:4, 1 Thessalonians 5:18).

5. **What are practical ways to cultivate a heart of worship?**

   - Spend daily time in prayer and praise, reflect on God's attributes, and serve others as an act of worship (Colossians 3:17, Psalm 29:2).

APPLICATIONS:

1. **Daily Praise**: Begin each day by thanking God for who He is and what He's done.

2. **Engage in Worship**: Participate actively in corporate worship, bringing your whole heart.

3. **Serve as Worship**: Choose an act of service this week as an offering of worship to God.

PRAYER PROMPTS:

1. Praise God for His greatness and holiness.
2. Thank Him for the privilege of worshiping Him in spirit and truth.
3. Ask for a heart that honors Him in every aspect of life.

Sola Scriptura 1:39

The Armor of God

FOCUS: EQUIPPING OURSELVES WITH THE SPIRITUAL TOOLS GOD PROVIDES TO STAND FIRM AGAINST THE SCHEMES OF THE ENEMY.

PRIMARY SCRIPTURE:

- Ephesians 6:10-18
- 2 Corinthians 10:3-5
- James 4:7

ADDITIONAL SCRIPTURE:

- 1 Thessalonians 5:8
- Romans 13:12
- Psalm 91:4
- Matthew 4:1-11

BIBLICAL TEACHING:

- The Armor of God equips believers to stand firm in spiritual warfare, emphasizing reliance on God's strength and truth (Ephesians 6:10-12).

- Each piece of the armor—truth, righteousness, readiness, faith, salvation, and the Word of God—addresses specific aspects of spiritual defense and offense (Ephesians 6:13-17).

- Prayer is integral to the armor, empowering believers to stay connected to God's strength and wisdom (Ephesians 6:18, James 4:7).

QUESTIONS AND ANSWERS:

1. **Why do believers need the Armor of God (Ephesians 6:11)?**

   - To stand against the devil's schemes and remain faithful in the face of spiritual attacks.

2. **What is the significance of each piece of the armor (Ephesians 6:14-17)?**

   - The belt of truth secures against lies, the breastplate of righteousness protects the heart, the shoes of peace enable readiness, the shield of faith extinguishes doubts, the helmet of salvation assures victory, and the sword of the Spirit wields God's Word against the enemy.

3. **How does prayer activate the Armor of God (Ephesians 6:18)?**

   - Prayer keeps believers connected to God, inviting His strength and guidance in battle.

4. **What can we learn from Jesus' response to temptation in Matthew 4:1-11?**

   - He used Scripture to counter lies, demonstrating the power of God's Word as a weapon in spiritual warfare.

5. **How can you ensure you are putting on the armor daily?**

   - By meditating on Scripture, walking in faith, praying consistently, and being aware of spiritual battles (Romans 13:12, Psalm 119:11).

APPLICATIONS:

1. **Pray Through the Armor**: Spend time each day intentionally praying through each piece of the Armor of God.

2. **Memorize Key Verses**: Learn verses that align with each piece of the armor to strengthen your defense against attacks.

3. **Resist the Enemy**: Identify areas of spiritual vulnerability and take steps to stand firm.

PRAYER PROMPTS:

1. Thank God for providing spiritual protection through His armor.

2. Pray for strength and discernment in spiritual battles.

3. Ask for wisdom to use Scripture effectively in times of temptation.

Sola Scriptura 1:40

Humility

FOCUS: CULTIVATING A HEART OF HUMILITY THAT REFLECTS CHRIST'S EXAMPLE AND GLORIFIES GOD.

PRIMARY SCRIPTURE:

- Philippians 2:3-8
- 1 Peter 5:5-6
- Micah 6:8

ADDITIONAL SCRIPTURE:

- James 4:10
- Matthew 23:11-12
- Proverbs 22:4
- John 13:12-15

BIBLICAL TEACHING:

- Humility involves recognizing our dependence on God, putting others above ourselves, and serving without seeking recognition (Philippians 2:3-4, James 4:10).

- Jesus exemplified humility through His incarnation, life, and sacrificial death (Philippians 2:5-8).

- God honors humility, while pride leads to downfall (1 Peter 5:5-6, Proverbs 22:4).

QUESTIONS AND ANSWERS:

1. **What does Philippians 2:3-4 teach about humility in relationships?**

   - It emphasizes valuing others above ourselves and avoiding selfish ambition.

2. **How did Jesus model humility in John 13:12-15?**

   - He humbled Himself by washing His disciples' feet, taking the role of a servant and teaching them to do the same.

3. **Why does God oppose the proud but give grace to the humble (1 Peter 5:5)?**

   - Pride exalts self over God, while humility acknowledges dependence on Him and aligns with His character.

4. **How can humility impact your daily decisions and interactions?**

   - It fosters patience, kindness, and a willingness to serve others without seeking recognition (Micah 6:8, Matthew 23:11).

5. **What practical steps can you take to grow in humility?**

   - Practice gratitude, seek accountability, and intentionally serve others in ways that don't draw attention (James 4:10, Romans 12:3).

APPLICATIONS:

1. **Serve Without Recognition**: Find a way to serve someone anonymously this week.

2. **Reflect on Christ's Example**: Meditate on Philippians 2:5-8 and consider how you can follow Jesus' humility.

3. **Practice Gratitude**: Regularly thank God for His blessings and recognize your dependence on Him.

PRAYER PROMPTS:

1. Thank God for Christ's example of humility and His grace toward the humble.

2. Pray for a heart that values others above self.

3. Ask God to reveal areas of pride and help you surrender them.

Sola Scriptura 1:41

The Fruit of the Spirit in Action

FOCUS: LIVING OUT THE FRUIT OF THE SPIRIT IN EVERYDAY LIFE AS EVIDENCE OF THE HOLY SPIRIT'S WORK.

PRIMARY SCRIPTURE:

- Galatians 5:22-23
- John 15:5
- Colossians 3:12-14

ADDITIONAL SCRIPTURE:

- Ephesians 4:2-3:
- Matthew 7:16-20
- James 3:17-18
- Philippians 1:9-11

BIBLICAL TEACHING:

- The Fruit of the Spirit is the visible evidence of a life transformed by Christ and guided by the Holy Spirit (Galatians 5:22-23).

- Living out the Fruit requires abiding in Christ and submitting to the Spirit's work in every area of life (John 15:5, Colossians 3:12).

- The Fruit of the Spirit demonstrates God's character to the world and brings unity, peace, and joy in relationships (Ephesians 4:2-3, Philippians 1:11).

QUESTIONS AND ANSWERS:

1. **What does it mean to bear the Fruit of the Spirit (Galatians 5:22-23)?**

   - It means displaying Christlike qualities that reflect the Spirit's work in your life.

2. **How does abiding in Christ help us bear fruit (John 15:5)?**

   - Remaining in Christ through prayer, Scripture, and obedience allows His life to flow through us, producing spiritual fruit.

3. **Which Fruit of the Spirit do you find most challenging, and why?**

   - Answers will vary, but growth requires prayer, surrender, and practice in that area (Philippians 1:9-11).

4. **How does the Fruit of the Spirit impact relationships?**

   - It fosters unity, forgiveness, and harmony, reflecting God's love and transforming communities (Colossians 3:12-14).

5. **What steps can you take to cultivate the Fruit of the Spirit?**

   - Meditate on Scripture, seek accountability, and pray for the Spirit's guidance in specific areas (Ephesians 4:2, James 3:17).

APPLICATIONS:

1. **Focus on Growth**: Identify one aspect of the Fruit of the Spirit to intentionally practice this week.

2. **Abide in Christ**: Set aside daily time for prayer and Scripture to deepen your connection with Him.

3. **Show Fruit in Action**: Serve someone in your life with love, kindness, or patience.

PRAYER PROMPTS:

1. Thank God for the Holy Spirit's work in producing fruit in your life.

2. Pray for growth in a specific area of the Fruit of the Spirit.

3. Ask for opportunities to demonstrate Christlike character in your relationships.

Sola Scriptura 1:42

The Fear of the Lord

FOCUS: EMBRACING REVERENCE AND AWE FOR GOD THAT LEADS TO WISDOM, OBEDIENCE, AND DEEPER WORSHIP.

PRIMARY SCRIPTURE:

- Proverbs 9:10
- Ecclesiastes 12:13
- Psalm 33:8

ADDITIONAL SCRIPTURE:

- Deuteronomy 10:12-13
- Isaiah 6:5
- Hebrews 12:28-29
- Matthew 10:28

BIBLICAL TEACHING:

- The fear of the Lord is a reverential awe of His holiness, power, and authority, leading to wisdom and obedience (Proverbs 9:10, Ecclesiastes 12:13).

- Fearing God involves recognizing His greatness and responding in worship, humility, and trust (Psalm 33:8, Isaiah 6:5).

- This fear motivates right living, aligning our lives with God's will and avoiding sin (Deuteronomy 10:12-13, Hebrews 12:28-29).

QUESTIONS AND ANSWERS:

1. **What does it mean to fear the Lord (Proverbs 9:10)?**

   - It means having deep reverence for God, acknowledging His holiness and authority, and living in a way that honors Him.

2. **How does the fear of the Lord lead to wisdom?**

   - Reverence for God shapes decisions, aligns priorities with His Word, and promotes humility (Proverbs 1:7, James 3:17).

3. **How did Isaiah respond to God's holiness (Isaiah 6:5)?**

   - He recognized his own sinfulness and responded with awe and repentance.

4. **How does fearing God impact your worship?**

   - It deepens reverence, gratitude, and awe for His greatness and grace (Psalm 33:8, Hebrews 12:28).

5. **What practical steps can you take to cultivate the fear of the Lord?**

   - Meditate on His attributes, pray for a heart of awe, and align your life with His commands (Deuteronomy 10:12-13, Matthew 10:28).

APPLICATIONS:

1. **Reflect on God's Holiness**: Spend time meditating on passages that describe God's holiness and greatness.

2. **Respond in Worship**: Incorporate reverence and awe into your worship, praising God for who He is.

3. **Live in Obedience**: Evaluate areas of your life where greater alignment with God's will is needed.

PRAYER PROMPTS:

1. Praise God for His holiness, power, and sovereignty.

2. Pray for a heart that reveres Him and seeks wisdom.

3. Ask for strength to live in obedience and awe of His greatness.

Sola Scriptura 1:43

God's Justice and Mercy

FOCUS: UNDERSTANDING THE BALANCE OF GOD'S JUSTICE AND MERCY AND HOW IT SHAPES OUR VIEW OF HIM AND OTHERS.

PRIMARY SCRIPTURE:

- Psalm 89:14
- Micah 6:8
- Romans 3:23-26

ADDITIONAL SCRIPTURE:

- Exodus 34:6-7
- Isaiah 30:18
- Matthew 5:7
- James 2:13

BIBLICAL TEACHING:

- God's justice ensures that sin is punished and His holiness upheld, while His mercy offers forgiveness and grace through Jesus Christ (Psalm 89:14, Romans 3:23-26).

- Justice and mercy are perfectly balanced in God's character, revealing His love and fairness (Exodus 34:6-7, Isaiah 30:18).

- Believers are called to reflect God's justice and mercy in their actions, treating others with fairness, compassion, and humility (Micah 6:8, Matthew 5:7).

QUESTIONS AND ANSWERS:

1. **How does God's justice and mercy meet at the cross (Romans 3:23-26)?**

   - God's justice is satisfied through Jesus' sacrifice, and His mercy is extended to sinners who trust in Him.

2. **What does it mean to act justly and love mercy (Micah 6:8)?**

   - It involves treating others fairly, showing compassion, and living with humility before God.

3. **How does God's justice and mercy impact your understanding of sin and grace?**

   - It highlights the seriousness of sin, the cost of grace, and the depth of God's love (Exodus 34:6-7, James 2:13).

4. **How can you reflect God's justice and mercy in your relationships?**

   - By advocating for fairness, forgiving others, and extending kindness, even when undeserved (Matthew 5:7, Colossians 3:12-13).

5. **Why is it important to trust in both God's justice and mercy?**

   - It assures us that wrongs will be righted while offering hope for forgiveness and restoration (Psalm 89:14, Isaiah 30:18).

APPLICATIONS:

1. **Show Mercy**: Forgive someone or show kindness where it is undeserved.

2. **Pursue Justice**: Support a cause or act that reflects God's justice.

3. **Thank God for Grace**: Reflect on the mercy you have received through Christ and thank Him in prayer.

PRAYER PROMPTS:

1. Thank God for His perfect balance of justice and mercy.

2. Pray for strength to reflect His character in your actions.

3. Ask for wisdom to respond with both fairness and compassion in challenging situations.

Sola Scriptura 1:44

The Sovereignty of God

FOCUS: TRUSTING IN GOD'S ABSOLUTE CONTROL AND PURPOSE IN ALL CIRCUMSTANCES.

PRIMARY SCRIPTURE:

- Isaiah 46:9-10
- Romans 8:28
- Daniel 4:35

ADDITIONAL SCRIPTURE:

- Psalm 115:3
- Proverbs 19:21
- Job 42:2
- Ephesians 1:11

BIBLICAL TEACHING:

- God's sovereignty means He reigns over all creation with absolute authority and control, ensuring His purposes are accomplished (Isaiah 46:10, Daniel 4:35).

- His sovereignty assures believers that all things, even suffering, are part of His redemptive plan (Romans 8:28, Ephesians 1:11).

- Trusting God's sovereignty leads to peace, humility, and confidence in His perfect will (Proverbs 19:21, Job 42:2).

QUESTIONS AND ANSWERS:

1. **What does it mean for God to be sovereign (Isaiah 46:9-10)?**

   - It means that God has ultimate authority and control over everything, and His plans cannot be thwarted.

2. **How does God's sovereignty provide comfort in difficult times (Romans 8:28)?**

   - It assures us that even hardships are part of His plan to bring good and accomplish His purposes.

3. **How does the sovereignty of God relate to human responsibility?**

   - God's sovereignty works in harmony with human choices, holding us accountable while fulfilling His purposes (Proverbs 16:9, Philippians 2:13).

4. **How can you grow in trusting God's sovereignty?**

   - By meditating on His promises, reflecting on His past faithfulness, and surrendering control to His will (Job 42:2, Psalm 115:3).

5. **How does acknowledging God's sovereignty impact your daily life?**

   - It brings peace, reduces anxiety, and encourages obedience and worship, knowing that God's purposes are good and perfect (Proverbs 19:21, Isaiah 26:3).

APPLICATIONS:

1. **Surrender Your Plans**: Bring a current struggle or decision to God, trusting His sovereign will.

2. **Reflect on God's Control**: Write down specific ways you've seen God's sovereignty in your life.

3. **Encourage Someone**: Share how trusting God's sovereignty has helped you in uncertain times.

PRAYER PROMPTS:

1. Praise God for His authority and control over all things.
2. Thank Him for working all things for good in your life.
3. Pray for trust and peace in areas where His sovereignty is hard to see.

Sola Scriptura 1:45

Biblical Leadership

FOCUS: EMBRACING SERVANT LEADERSHIP MODELED BY CHRIST AND EMPOWERED BY GOD'S WORD.

PRIMARY SCRIPTURE:

- Matthew 20:25-28
- 1 Timothy 3:1-7
- Titus 2:7-8

ADDITIONAL SCRIPTURE:

- Exodus 18:21
- 1 Peter 5:2-4
- Proverbs 16:12
- Philippians 2:3-4

BIBLICAL TEACHING:

- Biblical leadership is characterized by humility, servanthood, and a commitment to God's Word (Matthew 20:25-28, Philippians 2:3-4).

- Leaders are called to be examples in character and conduct, reflecting Christ's heart and priorities (1 Timothy 3:1-7, Titus 2:7-8).

- Godly leaders shepherd with integrity, protect those they lead, and point them to God's glory (1 Peter 5:2-4, Exodus 18:21).

QUESTIONS AND ANSWERS:

1. **What does it mean to be a servant leader (Matthew 20:25-28)?**

   - It means prioritizing the needs of others, serving with humility, and leading by example, as Christ did.

2. **What qualities should define a biblical leader (1 Timothy 3:1-7)?**

   - Leaders should be above reproach, self-controlled, gentle, and faithful in teaching, with integrity in their relationships.

3. **How can leaders guard against pride and self-interest (Philippians 2:3-4)?**

   - By focusing on the needs of others, staying rooted in Scripture, and regularly seeking God's guidance and accountability.

4. **Why is humility essential for leadership (1 Peter 5:2-3)?**

   - Humility ensures leaders depend on God, serve selflessly, and lead with grace and compassion.

5. **How can you lead in your own sphere of influence?**

   - By living with integrity, serving others, and pointing people to Christ through your words and actions (Titus 2:7-8).

APPLICATIONS:

1. **Model Christlike Leadership**: Identify one way you can lead by serving others this week.

2. **Evaluate Leadership**: Reflect on your leadership style and areas where humility and service can grow.

3. **Encourage Leaders**: Pray for and support leaders in your church or community.

PRAYER PROMPTS:

1. Thank God for the example of Christ's servant leadership.

2. Pray for humility and wisdom in any leadership roles you hold.

3. Ask God to raise up godly leaders in your church and community.

Sola Scriptura 1:46

Faith in God's Timing

FOCUS: TRUSTING GOD'S PERFECT TIMING AND PLAN IN ALL AREAS OF LIFE.

PRIMARY SCRIPTURE:

- Ecclesiastes 3:1-11
- Psalm 27:14
- Galatians 6:9

ADDITIONAL SCRIPTURE:

- Habakkuk 2:3
- Isaiah 40:31
- Lamentations 3:25-26
- Romans 8:25

BIBLICAL TEACHING:

- God's timing is perfect, even when it feels delayed or uncertain to us (Ecclesiastes 3:1-11, Habakkuk 2:3).

- Waiting on the Lord strengthens faith, develops patience, and aligns our hearts with His purposes (Psalm 27:14, Isaiah 40:31).

- Trusting God's timing helps us persevere in obedience and hope, knowing His promises are sure (Galatians 6:9, Romans 8:25).

QUESTIONS AND ANSWERS:

1. **How does Ecclesiastes 3:1-11 describe God's timing?**

- It highlights that every season and event has its purpose, orchestrated by God in His perfect timing.

2. **What are the benefits of waiting on the Lord (Isaiah 40:31)?**

   - Waiting renews strength, builds trust, and deepens reliance on God's power and faithfulness.

3. **How can believers remain patient in seasons of waiting (Psalm 27:14)?**

   - By seeking God in prayer, meditating on His promises, and trusting His faithfulness.

4. **Why does Galatians 6:9 encourage perseverance?**

   - It assures that faithful obedience will result in a harvest of blessings in God's time.

5. **How can trusting God's timing bring peace?**

   - It shifts focus from our uncertainties to God's sovereignty, allowing us to rest in His control (Romans 8:25, Lamentations 3:25-26).

APPLICATIONS:

1. **Trust in the Wait**: Identify an area where you are waiting on God and surrender it to Him in prayer.

2. **Persevere in Doing Good**: Continue serving faithfully, trusting that God's timing will bring results.

3. **Encourage Others**: Share a testimony of how trusting God's timing has brought peace or answered prayers.

PRAYER PROMPTS:

1. Thank God for His perfect timing and plans.

2. Pray for patience and trust in areas of waiting.

3. Ask for strength to persevere in obedience and hope.

Sola Scriptura 1:47

Spiritual Maturity

FOCUS: GROWING IN FAITH AND BECOMING MORE LIKE CHRIST THROUGH INTENTIONAL DISCIPLESHIP AND DEPENDENCE ON GOD.

PRIMARY SCRIPTURE:

- Hebrews 5:12-14
- Ephesians 4:13-15
- Philippians 3:12-14

ADDITIONAL SCRIPTURE:

- Colossians 1:28
- James 1:4
- 2 Timothy 3:16-17
- Galatians 5:22-23

BIBLICAL TEACHING:

- Spiritual maturity involves growing in faith, knowledge, and Christlikeness through consistent discipleship and application of God's Word (Hebrews 5:12-14, Ephesians 4:13).

- Maturity is marked by perseverance, discernment, and the Fruit of the Spirit, reflecting the transformation God works in His people (James 1:4, Galatians 5:22-23).

- Pursuing spiritual growth requires intentional effort, humility, and reliance on God's grace (Philippians 3:12-14, Colossians 1:28).

QUESTIONS AND ANSWERS:

1. **What are the marks of spiritual maturity (Hebrews 5:14, Galatians 5:22-23)?**

   - Discernment, perseverance, love, joy, peace, and other Christlike qualities evident in daily life.

2. **How does Ephesians 4:13-15 describe the goal of maturity?**

   - It is unity in faith, deeper knowledge of Christ, and living in a way that reflects His fullness.

3. **What role does Scripture play in spiritual growth (2 Timothy 3:16-17)?**

   - Scripture equips believers for good works, corrects errors, and provides wisdom for living.

4. **How can trials contribute to spiritual maturity (James 1:2-4)?**

   - Trials refine faith, develop perseverance, and shape character.

5. **What practical steps can you take to pursue maturity in Christ?**

   - Study Scripture, practice spiritual disciplines, seek mentorship, and actively apply God's truth in daily life.

APPLICATIONS:

1. **Set a Growth Goal**: Identify one area of your spiritual life to intentionally develop this month (e.g., prayer, Scripture study).

2. **Seek Accountability**: Partner with someone to encourage and challenge you in your walk with Christ.

3. **Live Out Maturity**: Take a step to apply God's Word in a specific situation this week.

PRAYER PROMPTS:

1. Thank God for His work in growing you toward maturity in Christ.

2. Pray for perseverance and discernment in your spiritual journey.

3. Ask for opportunities to mentor or encourage someone in their faith.

Sola Scriptura 1:48

God's Covenant Promises

FOCUS: TRUSTING IN GOD'S FAITHFULNESS AS REVEALED THROUGH HIS COVENANTS WITH HIS PEOPLE.

PRIMARY SCRIPTURE:

- Genesis 12:1-3
- Exodus 19:5-6
- Jeremiah 31:31-34

ADDITIONAL SCRIPTURE:

- Genesis 9:8-17
- 2 Samuel 7:12-16
- Luke 22:20
- Hebrews 8:6

BIBLICAL TEACHING:

- God's covenants demonstrate His faithfulness, revealing His redemptive plan through promises to Noah, Abraham, Israel, and David (Genesis 9:9, Genesis 12:3, 2 Samuel 7:12-16).

- The new covenant, fulfilled in Jesus, brings forgiveness, transformation, and eternal life (Jeremiah 31:31-34, Luke 22:20).

- Believers are called to live in light of God's covenant faithfulness, trusting His promises and participating in His mission (Hebrews 8:6, Exodus 19:6).

QUESTIONS AND ANSWERS:

1. **What does God's covenant with Abraham reveal about His plan (Genesis 12:1-3)?**

   - It shows God's intent to bless all nations through Abraham's descendants, ultimately fulfilled in Christ.

2. **How is the new covenant better than the old (Jeremiah 31:31-34, Hebrews 8:6)?**

   - The new covenant is written on hearts, offering complete forgiveness and a personal relationship with God through Christ.

3. **What is the significance of Jesus' words in Luke 22:20?**

   - Jesus established the new covenant through His sacrificial death, bringing salvation to all who believe.

4. **How can you trust in God's covenant promises today?**

   - By remembering His faithfulness throughout history and relying on His unchanging character (Hebrews 13:8, 2 Peter 1:4).

5. **What does it mean to live as part of God's covenant people (Exodus 19:5-6)?**

   - It means reflecting His holiness, sharing His love, and participating in His redemptive work.

APPLICATIONS:

1. **Reflect on God's Promises**: Write down specific promises from Scripture that remind you of His faithfulness.

2. **Live as a Covenant People**: Identify one way you can demonstrate God's love and truth to others this week.

3. **Trust in Christ**: Spend time thanking Jesus for fulfilling the covenant through His death and resurrection.

PRAYER PROMPTS:

1. Thank God for His faithfulness in keeping His covenant promises.

2. Praise Him for the new covenant through Jesus.

3. Pray for trust in His promises and strength to live as His covenant people.

Sola Scriptura 1:49

The Power of the Gospel

FOCUS: UNDERSTANDING THE TRANSFORMATIVE POWER OF THE GOSPEL FOR SALVATION AND DAILY LIVING.

PRIMARY SCRIPTURE:

- Romans 1:16
- 1 Corinthians 15:1-4
- 2 Corinthians 5:17

ADDITIONAL SCRIPTURE:

- John 3:16
- Ephesians 2:8-9
- Colossians 1:13-14
- Acts 4:12

BIBLICAL TEACHING:

- The gospel is the good news of Jesus' death and resurrection, bringing salvation, reconciliation, and transformation to all who believe (Romans 1:16, 1 Corinthians 15:1-4).

- It is the foundation of faith and the means by which believers are made new in Christ (2 Corinthians 5:17, Ephesians 2:8-9).

- The gospel empowers daily living, offering hope, freedom, and the call to share it with others (Colossians 1:13-14, Acts 4:12).

QUESTIONS AND ANSWERS:

1. **What is the core message of the gospel (1 Corinthians 15:1-4)?**

- Jesus died for our sins, was buried, and rose again, securing salvation for all who believe.

2. **How does the gospel bring transformation (2 Corinthians 5:17)?**

   - It makes believers new creations, breaking the power of sin and enabling them to live for God.

3. **Why is the gospel described as the power of God (Romans 1:16)?**

   - It brings salvation, changes hearts, and reveals God's righteousness and grace.

4. **What role does faith play in receiving the gospel (Ephesians 2:8-9)?**

   - Faith is the means by which we receive God's grace and are saved, not through works.

5. **How can you share the gospel with others?**

   - Through personal testimony, explaining Scripture, and living a life that reflects Christ's love and truth (John 3:16, 1 Peter 3:15).

APPLICATIONS:

1. **Reflect on the Gospel**: Spend time meditating on the message of the gospel and its impact on your life.

2. **Share the Good News**: Identify one person with whom you can share the gospel this week.

3. **Live the Gospel**: Let your actions and attitudes reflect the transformation the gospel brings.

PRAYER PROMPTS:

1. Praise God for the gift of the gospel and the salvation it brings.

2. Thank Jesus for His sacrifice and resurrection.

3. Pray for boldness and wisdom in sharing the gospel with others.

Sola Scriptura 1:50

The Role of Grace

FOCUS: UNDERSTANDING GOD'S UNMERITED FAVOR AND ITS TRANSFORMATIVE ROLE IN SALVATION, SANCTIFICATION, AND DAILY LIVING.

PRIMARY SCRIPTURE:

- Ephesians 2:8-9
- Titus 2:11-12
- 2 Corinthians 12:9

ADDITIONAL SCRIPTURE:

- Romans 6:14
- Hebrews 4:16
- John 1:16-17
- Romans 5:20-21

BIBLICAL TEACHING:

- Grace is God's unearned favor that brings salvation, empowers holy living, and sustains believers in weakness (Ephesians 2:8-9, 2 Corinthians 12:9).

- It frees us from the law's demands and enables us to live in obedience through the Spirit (Romans 6:14, Titus 2:11-12).

- Grace is both a gift to be received and a truth to be extended to others (Hebrews 4:16, John 1:16-17).

QUESTIONS AND ANSWERS:

1. **What is grace, and how does it bring salvation (Ephesians 2:8-9)?**
    - Grace is God's free gift of favor, offering salvation not through works but through faith in Christ.

2. **How does grace empower holy living (Titus 2:11-12)?**
    - Grace teaches us to renounce sin and live upright, godly lives as we rely on God's strength.

3. **Why does Paul describe grace as sufficient in 2 Corinthians 12:9?**
    - God's grace sustains us in our weakness, demonstrating His power and sufficiency in every situation.

4. **What is the relationship between grace and the law (Romans 6:14)?**
    - Grace liberates believers from the law's condemnation, enabling them to live under God's mercy and guidance.

5. **How can believers extend grace to others?**
    - By forgiving, showing kindness, and reflecting God's love in relationships (Colossians 3:13, Matthew 5:7).

APPLICATIONS:

1. **Reflect on Grace**: Meditate on ways God's grace has transformed your life.

2. **Extend Grace**: Identify someone who needs forgiveness or encouragement and offer grace to them.

3. **Rely on Grace**: Surrender an area of weakness or struggle to God's sustaining grace.

PRAYER PROMPTS:

1. Thank God for the gift of grace in salvation and daily life.
2. Pray for strength to live in the power of God's grace.
3. Ask for a heart that extends grace to others generously.

Sola Scriptura 1:51

The Pursuit of Holiness

FOCUS: UNDERSTANDING GOD'S CALL TO HOLINESS AND ACTIVELY PURSUING A LIFE SET APART FOR HIS GLORY.

PRIMARY SCRIPTURE:

- 1 Peter 1:15-16
- Hebrews 12:14
- Romans 12:1-2

ADDITIONAL SCRIPTURE:

- Leviticus 20:26
- 2 Corinthians 7:1
- 1 Thessalonians 4:3-7
- Matthew 5:48

BIBLICAL TEACHING:

- Holiness is being set apart for God's purposes, reflecting His character through purity, obedience, and devotion (1 Peter 1:15-16, Leviticus 20:26).

- It requires active effort, relying on God's Spirit to transform thoughts, desires, and actions (Romans 12:1-2, 2 Corinthians 7:1).

- The pursuit of holiness honors God and enables deeper fellowship with Him (Hebrews 12:14, 1 Thessalonians 4:7).

QUESTIONS AND ANSWERS:

1. **What does it mean to be holy (1 Peter 1:15-16)?**

- It means living in a way that reflects God's purity and separateness from sin.

2. **Why is holiness essential for believers (Hebrews 12:14)?**

   - Without holiness, believers cannot experience the fullness of God's presence or witness effectively to others.

3. **How can believers pursue holiness in daily life (Romans 12:1-2)?**

   - By surrendering to God, renewing their minds with Scripture, and resisting conformity to the world.

4. **What role does the Holy Spirit play in holiness?**

   - The Spirit empowers believers to resist sin, grow in Christlikeness, and fulfill God's purposes (Galatians 5:16, 2 Corinthians 3:18).

5. **How does holiness impact relationships with others?**

   - It promotes integrity, love, and peace, reflecting God's character in interactions (1 Thessalonians 4:3-6, Matthew 5:9).

APPLICATIONS:

1. **Identify Barriers**: Examine your life for areas that hinder holiness and commit to change.

2. **Renew Your Mind**: Spend focused time in Scripture and prayer to align your thoughts with God's truth.

3. **Seek Accountability**: Partner with someone to encourage mutual growth in holiness.

PRAYER PROMPTS:

1. Praise God for His holiness and the call to reflect His character.

2. Pray for strength and perseverance in pursuing holiness.

3. Ask for the Spirit's help in overcoming specific sins or struggles.

Sola Scriptura 1:52

The Body of Christ

FOCUS: EMBRACING THE UNITY AND DIVERSITY OF THE CHURCH AS THE BODY OF CHRIST, WORKING TOGETHER TO GLORIFY GOD.

PRIMARY SCRIPTURE:

- 1 Corinthians 12:12-27
- Ephesians 4:11-13
- Romans 12:4-5

ADDITIONAL SCRIPTURE:

- Colossians 1:18
- Hebrews 10:24-25
- 1 Peter 4:10
- Acts 2:42-47

BIBLICAL TEACHING:

- The Church is the Body of Christ, with each member uniquely gifted to serve and build up the whole (1 Corinthians 12:12-27, Romans 12:4-5).

- Unity in the Body reflects Christ's love and glorifies God, even amid diversity (Ephesians 4:11-13, Colossians 1:18).

- Believers are called to actively participate in the Church, encouraging and supporting one another in faith (Hebrews 10:24-25, Acts 2:42-47).

QUESTIONS AND ANSWERS:

1. **What does it mean to be part of the Body of Christ (1 Corinthians 12:12-27)?**

   - It means belonging to a community where every member has a unique role and contributes to the whole.

2. **How do spiritual gifts equip the Body of Christ (Ephesians 4:11-13)?**

   - They build unity, maturity, and effectiveness in the Church's mission.

3. **Why is unity important in the Body of Christ (Romans 12:4-5)?**

   - Unity demonstrates God's love, strengthens believers, and advances His kingdom.

4. **What role does fellowship play in the life of the Church (Acts 2:42-47)?**

   - Fellowship fosters growth, support, and shared worship, reflecting God's design for community.

5. **How can you contribute to the health of the Body of Christ?**

   - By using your gifts, encouraging others, and committing to the Church's mission and unity (1 Peter 4:10, Hebrews 10:24).

APPLICATIONS:

1. **Use Your Gifts**: Identify and actively use your spiritual gifts to serve in your church.

2. **Foster Unity**: Seek opportunities to build relationships and encourage others in your faith community.

3. **Participate Fully**: Commit to regular involvement in worship, fellowship, and service.

PRAYER PROMPTS:

1. Thank God for the gift of the Church and its unity in Christ.
2. Pray for wisdom to use your gifts to build up the Body of Christ.
3. Ask for strength to foster unity and serve faithfully in your church community.

Sola Scriptura 1:53

The Call to Mission

FOCUS: EMBRACING THE BELIEVER'S RESPONSIBILITY TO SHARE THE GOSPEL AND LIVE AS AMBASSADORS FOR CHRIST.

PRIMARY SCRIPTURE:

- Matthew 28:19-20
- Acts 1:8
- 2 Corinthians 5:20

ADDITIONAL SCRIPTURE:

- Romans 10:14-15
- 1 Peter 3:15
- John 20:21
- Isaiah 6:8

BIBLICAL TEACHING:

- The Great Commission calls all believers to share the gospel, making disciples of all nations (Matthew 28:19-20, Acts 1:8).

- As ambassadors of Christ, believers represent Him in their words and actions, calling others to reconciliation with God (2 Corinthians 5:20, John 20:21).

- Mission begins locally but extends globally, requiring a heart of obedience and reliance on the Holy Spirit (Romans 10:14, Isaiah 6:8).

QUESTIONS AND ANSWERS:

1. **What is the Great Commission, and why is it important (Matthew 28:19-20)?**

   - It is Jesus' command to share the gospel and make disciples, fulfilling God's plan to bring salvation to the world.

2. **How does Acts 1:8 guide believers in their mission?**

   - It emphasizes being witnesses locally, regionally, and globally, empowered by the Holy Spirit.

3. **What does it mean to be an ambassador for Christ (2 Corinthians 5:20)?**

   - Representing Christ by sharing His message of reconciliation and living as a reflection of His love and truth.

4. **What are practical ways to engage in mission today?**

   - Sharing your testimony, supporting missions, mentoring new believers, and serving in your local community.

5. **How can you overcome fear or hesitation in sharing the gospel (1 Peter 3:15)?**

   - By trusting in God's power, preparing to share your faith, and praying for boldness and opportunities.

APPLICATIONS:

1. **Identify Your Mission Field**: Consider where God has placed you and how you can share the gospel there.

2. **Prepare Your Testimony**: Practice sharing your story of faith in a concise and relatable way.

3. **Pray for Opportunities**: Ask God to open doors for you to share the gospel and serve others.

PRAYER PROMPTS:

1. Thank God for the privilege of being part of His mission.

2. Pray for boldness and wisdom in sharing the gospel.

3. Ask for open hearts and opportunities to reach others with Christ's love.

Sola Scriptura 1:54

The Promises of Heaven

FOCUS: MEDITATING ON THE HOPE AND JOY OF ETERNITY WITH GOD AND ITS IMPACT ON LIFE TODAY.

PRIMARY SCRIPTURE:

- Revelation 21:1-4
- John 14:1-3
- Philippians 3:20-21

ADDITIONAL SCRIPTURE:

- 2 Corinthians 4:17-18
- 1 Thessalonians 4:16-17
- Matthew 6:19-21
- Hebrews 13:14

BIBLICAL TEACHING:

- Heaven is the believer's eternal home, where God dwells with His people, bringing perfect joy, peace, and freedom from pain (Revelation 21:1-4, John 14:1-3).

- This hope sustains believers in trials, reminding them of the eternal glory that far outweighs earthly suffering (2 Corinthians 4:17-18, Philippians 3:20-21).

- Living with heaven in view shapes priorities, encouraging faithfulness, generosity, and eternal-mindedness (Matthew 6:19-21, Hebrews 13:14).

QUESTIONS AND ANSWERS:

1. **What does Revelation 21:1-4 teach about the promises of heaven?**

   - It describes a renewed creation where God dwells with His people, erasing all sorrow, pain, and death.

2. **How does Jesus' promise in John 14:1-3 provide comfort?**

   - It assures believers of a place prepared for them and the certainty of being with Him forever.

3. **How can the hope of heaven sustain believers during trials (2 Corinthians 4:17-18)?**

   - It reminds them that earthly troubles are temporary and lead to eternal glory.

4. **What does it mean to store treasures in heaven (Matthew 6:19-21)?**

   - It means investing in eternal values like faith, love, and service rather than temporary material wealth.

5. **How can living with a heavenly perspective impact daily life?**

   - It fosters peace, hope, and motivation to prioritize God's kingdom and live faithfully (Philippians 3:20-21, Hebrews 13:14).

APPLICATIONS:

1. **Meditate on Heaven**: Spend time reflecting on Scripture passages about heaven and eternal life.

2. **Live with Eternal Priorities**: Choose one area of your life to align more closely with heavenly values.

3. **Share the Hope of Heaven**: Encourage someone by sharing the promises of eternity with God.

PRAYER PROMPTS:

1. Thank God for the promise of eternal life and the joy of heaven.

2. Pray for a heart focused on eternal priorities.

3. Ask for opportunities to share the hope of heaven with others.

Sola Scriptura 1:55

The Peace of God

FOCUS: EMBRACING THE PEACE THAT COMES FROM TRUSTING GOD IN EVERY CIRCUMSTANCE.

PRIMARY SCRIPTURE:

- Philippians 4:6-7
- Isaiah 26:3
- John 14:27

ADDITIONAL SCRIPTURE:

- Colossians 3:15
- Psalm 46:10
- Romans 5:1
- Matthew 11:28-30

BIBLICAL TEACHING:

- The peace of God is a gift that surpasses human understanding, guarding the hearts and minds of those who trust in Him (Philippians 4:6-7, Isaiah 26:3).
- True peace comes from Jesus, who reconciles us to God and provides rest for our souls (John 14:27, Matthew 11:28).
- Living in God's peace requires surrender, prayer, and trust in His sovereignty (Colossians 3:15, Psalm 46:10).

QUESTIONS AND ANSWERS:

1. **What is the peace of God, and how does it differ from worldly peace (John 14:27)?**

- It is an inner calm and assurance rooted in Christ, unaffected by external circumstances.

2. **How does Philippians 4:6-7 teach us to experience God's peace?**

- Through prayer, thanksgiving, and trusting God with our anxieties, His peace guards our hearts and minds.

3. **What role does trust play in experiencing God's peace (Isaiah 26:3)?**

- Trusting in God keeps our minds steadfast, allowing His peace to sustain us.

4. **How can believers let the peace of Christ rule in their hearts (Colossians 3:15)?**

- By surrendering control, focusing on God's promises, and fostering unity with others.

5. **How does peace with God (Romans 5:1) impact daily life?**

- It frees us from guilt and fear, providing confidence in God's love and guidance.

APPLICATIONS:

1. **Surrender Your Worries**: Identify one area of anxiety and give it to God in prayer.

2. **Focus on God's Promises**: Memorize a Scripture about peace and meditate on it during stressful times.

3. **Cultivate Stillness**: Set aside time to be quiet before God, reflecting on His presence and sovereignty.

PRAYER PROMPTS:

1. Thank God for the gift of peace through Christ.

2. Pray for trust and surrender in areas of worry or stress.

3. Ask for opportunities to share God's peace with others.

Sola Scriptura 1:56

Christian Contentment

FOCUS: FINDING SATISFACTION IN GOD'S PROVISION AND TRUSTING HIM IN EVERY CIRCUMSTANCE.

PRIMARY SCRIPTURE:

- Philippians 4:11-13
- 1 Timothy 6:6-8
- Hebrews 13:5

ADDITIONAL SCRIPTURE:

- Psalm 23:1
- Matthew 6:25-34
- Proverbs 30:8-9
- **Luke 12:15**

BIBLICAL TEACHING:

- Contentment is a learned attitude of trusting God's provision and finding satisfaction in Him, regardless of circumstances (Philippians 4:11-13, 1 Timothy 6:6).

- True contentment is rooted in God's presence and promises, freeing believers from greed and fear (Hebrews 13:5, Psalm 23:1).

- It involves shifting focus from earthly possessions to eternal priorities (Matthew 6:33, Luke 12:15).

QUESTIONS AND ANSWERS:

1. **What is the "secret" of contentment Paul describes in Philippians 4:11-13?**

- It is reliance on Christ's strength, trusting Him in both abundance and need.

2. **How does godliness lead to contentment (1 Timothy 6:6)?**

   - Godliness aligns our desires with God's will, teaching us to be satisfied with His provision.

3. **What role does gratitude play in contentment?**

   - Gratitude shifts focus from what we lack to recognizing God's blessings and faithfulness (1 Thessalonians 5:18).

4. **How can believers guard against discontentment (Hebrews 13:5)?**

   - By trusting God's promise never to leave or forsake them and focusing on His sufficiency.

5. **What practical steps can you take to grow in contentment?**

   - Practice gratitude, limit comparisons, and focus on eternal treasures rather than material wealth (Matthew 6:19-20).

APPLICATIONS:

1. **Practice Gratitude**: Write down three things you are thankful for each day this week.

2. **Simplify**: Evaluate areas of excess in your life and focus on what truly matters.

3. **Trust God's Provision**: Reflect on ways God has provided for you in the past and trust Him for the future.

PRAYER PROMPTS:

1. Thank God for His provision and faithfulness.

2. Pray for contentment in areas where you feel lack or comparison.

3. Ask for a heart that treasures God above all else.

147

Sola Scriptura 1:57

The Joy of the Lord

FOCUS: UNDERSTANDING THE JOY THAT COMES FROM KNOWING GOD AND LIVING IN HIS PRESENCE.

PRIMARY SCRIPTURE:

- Nehemiah 8:10
- Psalm 16:11
- Philippians 4:4

ADDITIONAL SCRIPTURE:

- John 15:11
- Romans 15:13
- James 1:2-3
- Isaiah 61:10

BIBLICAL TEACHING:

- Joy is a fruit of the Spirit and a deep, abiding sense of well-being that comes from God's presence and promises (Psalm 16:11, Romans 15:13).

- The joy of the Lord provides strength in trials, reminding believers of their identity and hope in Christ (Nehemiah 8:10, James 1:2-3).

- Rejoicing in the Lord is a command and a privilege, rooted in gratitude and trust in His goodness (Philippians 4:4, John 15:11).

QUESTIONS AND ANSWERS:

1. **What is the "joy of the Lord" described in Nehemiah 8:10?**

- It is the strength and encouragement believers find in God's presence and promises.

2. **How does Psalm 16:11 describe the source of true joy?**

   - True joy is found in God's presence and the eternal pleasures He provides.

3. **What does it mean to rejoice always (Philippians 4:4)?**

   - It means maintaining a heart of gratitude and trust in God, regardless of circumstances.

4. **How can joy and trials coexist (James 1:2-3)?**

   - Trials deepen faith and reliance on God, producing lasting joy in His work within us.

5. **What practical steps can you take to cultivate joy in your life?**

   - Spend time in worship, reflect on God's blessings, and rely on the Holy Spirit for strength and peace (Romans 15:13).

APPLICATIONS:

1. **Practice Joyful Worship**: Dedicate time to praising God for His goodness.

2. **Reflect on Blessings**: Write down ways God has been faithful and how His presence brings joy.

3. **Encourage Others**: Share a testimony of how God has brought joy in your life, even in difficult times.

PRAYER PROMPTS:

1. Thank God for the gift of joy through His presence and promises.

2. Pray for strength and joy in trials or challenging circumstances.

3. Ask for opportunities to share His joy with others.

Sola Scriptura 1:58

The Power of Prayer

FOCUS: RECOGNIZING PRAYER AS A VITAL CONNECTION WITH GOD THAT TRANSFORMS LIVES AND CIRCUMSTANCES.

PRIMARY SCRIPTURE:

- James 5:16
- Philippians 4:6-7
- Matthew 7:7-8

ADDITIONAL SCRIPTURE:

- 1 Thessalonians 5:16-18
- Mark 11:24
- Ephesians 6:18
- Luke 18:1-8

BIBLICAL TEACHING:

- Prayer is a powerful way to communicate with God, bringing peace, guidance, and transformation (Philippians 4:6-7, James 5:16).

- God invites believers to approach Him boldly and persistently, trusting His faithfulness and timing (Matthew 7:7-8, Luke 18:1-8).

- Through prayer, believers align their hearts with God's will and experience His presence and power in their lives (Ephesians 6:18, 1 Thessalonians 5:17).

QUESTIONS AND ANSWERS:

1. **What makes prayer powerful and effective (James 5:16)?**

   - Prayer rooted in faith and righteousness connects us to God's power and purposes.

2. **How does Philippians 4:6-7 encourage prayer during anxiety?**

   - It teaches that presenting requests to God with thanksgiving brings peace that guards hearts and minds.

3. **Why does Jesus emphasize persistence in prayer (Luke 18:1-8)?**

   - Persistence demonstrates faith and trust in God's character and timing.

4. **What role does the Holy Spirit play in prayer (Ephesians 6:18)?**

   - The Spirit guides, intercedes, and empowers believers to pray according to God's will.

5. **How can you make prayer a consistent part of your life?**

   - Set aside regular times for prayer, incorporate prayer into daily activities, and stay attuned to God's presence (1 Thessalonians 5:17).

APPLICATIONS:

1. **Pray with Purpose**: Identify a specific situation or person to pray for daily this week.

2. **Develop a Prayer Habit**: Set a consistent time each day to focus on prayer.

3. **Trust in God's Timing**: Reflect on past answered prayers and thank God for His faithfulness.

PRAYER PROMPTS:

1. Praise God for His invitation to come to Him in prayer.

2. Pray for strength to trust Him in unanswered prayers.

3. Ask for a deeper connection with Him through consistent prayer.

Sola Scriptura 1:59

Living as Salt and Light

FOCUS: EMBRACING THE BELIEVER'S ROLE IN INFLUENCING THE WORLD FOR CHRIST THROUGH WITNESS AND GOOD WORKS.

PRIMARY SCRIPTURE:

- Matthew 5:13-16
- Philippians 2:14-16
- 1 Peter 2:12

ADDITIONAL SCRIPTURE:

- Colossians 4:5-6
- Ephesians 5:8-10
- Romans 12:21
- Proverbs 4:18

BIBLICAL TEACHING:

- Believers are called to be salt, preserving goodness and enhancing the world, and light, revealing truth and pointing others to Christ (Matthew 5:13-16, Colossians 4:5-6).

- Living as salt and light involves integrity, good works, and boldness in sharing the gospel (Philippians 2:14-16, 1 Peter 2:12).

- This role requires reliance on God's power, avoiding compromise, and staying true to His Word (Ephesians 5:8-10, Romans 12:21).

QUESTIONS AND ANSWERS:

1. **What does it mean to be the salt of the earth (Matthew 5:13)?**

   - It means preserving goodness, influencing culture positively, and living out Christ's values.

2. **How can believers shine as light in the world (Matthew 5:14-16)?**

   - By reflecting God's truth and love, doing good works, and sharing the gospel boldly.

3. **How does Philippians 2:14-16 encourage believers to live differently?**

   - It challenges believers to stand out through purity, integrity, and offering hope in a dark world.

4. **What practical ways can you live as salt and light in your community?**

   - Serve others, speak with kindness, uphold truth, and engage in acts of compassion.

5. **How can you avoid losing your saltiness or dimming your light?**

   - Stay rooted in Scripture, maintain accountability, and rely on the Holy Spirit for boldness and wisdom.

APPLICATIONS:

1. **Engage Your Community**: Find one way to serve or bless your local community this week.

2. **Live with Integrity**: Commit to reflecting Christ in your actions, words, and decisions.

3. **Share Your Light**: Look for an opportunity to share your faith with someone.

PRAYER PROMPTS:

1. Ask God to help you be salt and light in your relationships and community.

2. Pray for boldness to reflect Christ through good works and truth.

3. Thank Him for the privilege of being His representative in the world.

Sola Scriptura 1:60

The Victory of the Cross

FOCUS: UNDERSTANDING THE TRIUMPH OF CHRIST'S DEATH AND RESURRECTION OVER SIN, DEATH, AND SATAN.

PRIMARY SCRIPTURE:

- Colossians 2:13-15
- 1 Corinthians 15:55-57
- Romans 8:37

ADDITIONAL SCRIPTURE:

- John 19:30
- Hebrews 2:14-15
- Revelation 12:10-11
- Isaiah 53:5

BIBLICAL TEACHING:

- The cross is the ultimate symbol of victory, where Jesus paid the penalty for sin, conquered death, and disarmed spiritual powers (Colossians 2:13-15, 1 Corinthians 15:55-57).

- Christ's victory gives believers freedom, assurance, and the power to live as conquerors through His love (Romans 8:37, Hebrews 2:14-15).

- The resurrection confirms Jesus' triumph and secures eternal hope for all who trust in Him (John 19:30, Revelation 12:10-11).

QUESTIONS AND ANSWERS:

1. **What does it mean that Jesus triumphed over powers and authorities (Colossians 2:15)?**

   - He defeated Satan and all spiritual forces, stripping them of their power to condemn believers.

2. **How does 1 Corinthians 15:55-57 describe the victory of the cross?**

   - It celebrates Christ's triumph over death, granting believers eternal life and victory through Him.

3. **What does Jesus' declaration "It is finished" mean (John 19:30)?**

   - It signifies the completion of His mission to redeem humanity, paying the full penalty for sin.

4. **How does the victory of the cross empower believers today (Romans 8:37)?**

   - It assures them they can overcome sin, fear, and trials through Christ's love and strength.

5. **How can you live in light of Christ's victory?**

   - By embracing freedom from sin, standing firm in spiritual battles, and sharing the hope of the gospel with others.

APPLICATIONS:

1. **Live in Freedom**: Reflect on areas where you need to embrace the victory of the cross and surrender sin or fear.

2. **Celebrate the Cross**: Spend time in worship, thanking Jesus for His sacrifice and triumph.

3. **Share the Victory**: Tell someone about the hope and freedom found in Christ's victory.

PRAYER PROMPTS:

1. Praise Jesus for His triumph over sin, death, and Satan.
2. Thank Him for the freedom and hope His victory brings.
3. Pray for strength to live boldly in light of the cross.

Sola Scriptura 1:61
The Return of Christ

FOCUS: UNDERSTANDING THE PROMISE OF JESUS' RETURN AND HOW IT SHAPES THE BELIEVER'S LIFE.

PRIMARY SCRIPTURE:

- Matthew 24:30-31
- 1 Thessalonians 4:16-17
- Revelation 22:12

ADDITIONAL SCRIPTURE:

- Acts 1:11
- 2 Peter 3:10-13
- Titus 2:13
- Matthew 25:1-13

BIBLICAL TEACHING:

- Jesus' return is a core Christian hope, where He will come in glory to judge the living and the dead, and establish His eternal kingdom (Matthew 24:30-31, Acts 1:11).

- Believers are called to live in readiness, anticipating His return with faithfulness and holiness (Matthew 25:1-13, Titus 2:13).

- The certainty of Christ's return inspires perseverance, evangelism, and focus on eternal priorities (2 Peter 3:10-13, Revelation 22:12).

QUESTIONS AND ANSWERS:

1. **What does Scripture teach about the manner of Jesus' return (Matthew 24:30-31)?**

   - It will be visible, powerful, and glorious, as Jesus gathers His followers and establishes His reign.

2. **How does the promise of Christ's return impact daily life (Titus 2:13)?**

   - It encourages hope, motivates holiness, and reminds believers to live for eternal values.

3. **Why does Jesus warn about being ready in Matthew 25:1-13?**

   - To highlight the importance of spiritual preparedness, as the exact time of His return is unknown.

4. **What are the signs of Christ's return described in Scripture (Matthew 24:4-14)?**

   - They include wars, natural disasters, moral decay, persecution, and the spread of the gospel.

5. **How can you live in readiness for Jesus' return?**

   - By growing in faith, sharing the gospel, and living a life that honors God (2 Peter 3:11-12, 1 Thessalonians 5:6).

APPLICATIONS:

1. **Evaluate Your Priorities**: Reflect on whether your life reflects readiness for Christ's return.

2. **Share the Hope**: Talk to someone about the promise of Jesus' return and its importance.

3. **Focus on Eternal Values**: Identify one area where you can prioritize God's kingdom over worldly concerns.

PRAYER PROMPTS:

1. Thank God for the promise of Christ's return and the hope it provides.

2. Pray for strength to live faithfully in anticipation of Jesus' return.

3. Intercede for those who do not yet know Christ, that they may come to faith before His return.

Sola Scriptura 1:62
God's Unchanging Character

FOCUS: TRUSTING IN GOD'S FAITHFULNESS AND CONSTANCY IN AN EVER-CHANGING WORLD.

PRIMARY SCRIPTURE:

- Malachi 3:6
- Hebrews 13:8
- James 1:17

ADDITIONAL SCRIPTURE:

- Psalm 102:25-27
- Numbers 23:19
- Isaiah 40:8
- Lamentations 3:22-23

BIBLICAL TEACHING:

- God's unchanging character provides a foundation for faith, as His promises, love, and purposes remain constant (Malachi 3:6, James 1:17).

- In a world of uncertainty, God's immutability assures believers of His reliability and trustworthiness (Hebrews 13:8, Numbers 23:19).

- His unchanging nature inspires worship, hope, and confidence, especially in times of change or trial (Psalm 102:25-27, Isaiah 40:8).

QUESTIONS AND ANSWERS:

1. **What does it mean that God does not change (Malachi 3:6)?**

   - It means His nature, character, and promises remain constant, providing a firm foundation for faith.

2. **How does Hebrews 13:8 bring comfort in changing circumstances?**

   - It assures us that Jesus' love, grace, and power are unchanging and reliable.

3. **Why is God's unchanging nature essential for trust (Numbers 23:19)?**

   - It means His promises are certain, and He is completely faithful in all He says and does.

4. **How can believers rely on God's unchanging Word (Isaiah 40:8)?**

   - By meditating on Scripture, which endures forever and provides guidance and hope.

5. **What practical steps can you take to focus on God's constancy in uncertain times?**

   - Spend time in prayer, reflect on His promises, and worship Him for His faithfulness (Lamentations 3:22-23).

APPLICATIONS:

1. **Anchor in Scripture**: Memorize a verse about God's unchanging character to meditate on in uncertain times.

2. **Reflect on God's Faithfulness**: Write down ways God has shown His constancy in your life.

3. **Encourage Someone**: Share the comfort of God's unchanging nature with someone facing uncertainty.

PRAYER PROMPTS:

1. Praise God for being unchanging and faithful in all His ways.

2. Thank Him for the security and hope His constancy provides.

3. Pray for trust and confidence in His unchanging character during life's challenges.

Sola Scriptura 1:63
God's Love for the World

FOCUS: UNDERSTANDING THE DEPTH OF GOD'S LOVE FOR HUMANITY AND HOW BELIEVERS CAN REFLECT IT IN THEIR LIVES.

PRIMARY SCRIPTURE:

- John 3:16
- 1 John 4:9-10
- Romans 5:8

ADDITIONAL SCRIPTURE:

- Ephesians 2:4-5
- Psalm 103:11-12
- Isaiah 49:15-16
- Matthew 22:37-39

BIBLICAL TEACHING:

- God's love for the world is sacrificial, unconditional, and redemptive, demonstrated through the gift of His Son, Jesus Christ (John 3:16, Romans 5:8).

- His love reaches beyond human failure, offering forgiveness and reconciliation to all who believe (Ephesians 2:4-5, Psalm 103:11-12).

- Believers are called to embody God's love by loving Him fully and extending His love to others (Matthew 22:37-39, 1 John 4:11).

QUESTIONS AND ANSWERS:

1. **What does John 3:16 reveal about the nature of God's love?**

   - It is universal, sacrificial, and seeks the redemption of all who believe in Jesus.

2. **How does Romans 5:8 demonstrate the depth of God's love?**

   - It shows that God loved us even in our sin, giving His Son to reconcile us to Himself.

3. **What does it mean to love others as God loves us (1 John 4:11)?**

   - It involves selflessness, forgiveness, and actively seeking the good of others, reflecting Christ's love.

4. **How can believers grow in their understanding of God's love?**

   - Through prayer, studying Scripture, and experiencing His love in daily life (Ephesians 3:17-19).

5. **What practical steps can you take to reflect God's love to the world?**

   - Show kindness, share the gospel, and serve those in need, following Jesus' example (Matthew 22:39, John 13:34-35).

APPLICATIONS:

1. **Reflect on God's Love**: Spend time meditating on Scriptures about God's love and thanking Him for it.

2. **Show Love in Action**: Identify someone who needs encouragement or support and show them God's love.

3. **Share the Gospel**: Look for an opportunity to share the message of God's love with someone.

PRAYER PROMPTS:

1. Praise God for His unfailing, sacrificial love.

2. Pray for a deeper understanding of His love and how to reflect it.

3. Ask for opportunities to demonstrate God's love to others.

Sola Scriptura 1:64
Walking in the Spirit

FOCUS: LIVING A LIFE EMPOWERED AND DIRECTED BY THE HOLY SPIRIT.

PRIMARY SCRIPTURE:

- Galatians 5:16-17
- Romans 8:14
- John 16:13

ADDITIONAL SCRIPTURE:

- Ephesians 5:18
- Acts 1:8
- 2 Corinthians 3:17-18
- 1 Corinthians 2:12

BIBLICAL TEACHING:

- Walking in the Spirit means living under the Spirit's guidance, relying on His power to resist sin and grow in Christlikeness (Galatians 5:16-17, John 16:13).

- The Spirit empowers believers to live boldly, understand God's truth, and reflect Christ to the world (Romans 8:14, Acts 1:8).

- A Spirit-filled life produces fruit, transformation, and greater intimacy with God (Ephesians 5:18, 2 Corinthians 3:17-18).

QUESTIONS AND ANSWERS:

1. **What does it mean to walk by the Spirit (Galatians 5:16)?**

   - It means living in step with the Spirit's guidance, rejecting sinful desires, and pursuing righteousness.

2. **How does the Spirit guide believers into truth (John 16:13)?**

   - The Spirit illuminates Scripture, provides discernment, and reveals God's will.

3. **What are the fruits of walking in the Spirit (Galatians 5:22-23)?**

   - Love, joy, peace, patience, kindness, goodness, faithfulness, gentleness, and self-control.

4. **How can believers be filled with the Spirit (Ephesians 5:18)?**

   - Through prayer, surrender, worship, and reliance on the Spirit's power.

5. **What practical steps can you take to live a Spirit-led life?**

   - Spend time in prayer, seek the Spirit's guidance in decisions, and cultivate spiritual disciplines (Romans 8:5-6).

APPLICATIONS:

1. **Seek the Spirit's Guidance**: Pray specifically for the Spirit to lead you in a current decision or challenge.

2. **Evaluate Your Walk**: Reflect on areas where you need to rely more on the Spirit's power.

3. **Bear Fruit**: Focus on living out one aspect of the Fruit of the Spirit this week.

PRAYER PROMPTS:

1. Thank God for the gift of the Holy Spirit as a guide and helper.

2. Pray for sensitivity to the Spirit's leading in your life.

3. Ask for boldness to live a Spirit-empowered life.

Sola Scriptura 1:65
The Cost of Discipleship

FOCUS: EMBRACING THE SACRIFICES AND REWARDS OF FOLLOWING JESUS WHOLEHEARTEDLY.

PRIMARY SCRIPTURE:

- Luke 14:27-33
- Matthew 16:24-25
- Philippians 3:7-8

ADDITIONAL SCRIPTURE:

- Mark 10:29-30
- John 15:18-20
- 2 Timothy 3:12
- Revelation 2:10

BIBLICAL TEACHING:

- Following Jesus requires self-denial, commitment, and a willingness to endure suffering for His sake (Luke 14:27, Matthew 16:24).

- True discipleship values Christ above all, recognizing that any earthly loss is outweighed by the eternal reward of knowing Him (Philippians 3:7-8, Mark 10:29-30).

- The cost of discipleship is real, but so are the blessings of intimacy with Christ and the hope of eternal life (John 15:18-20, Revelation 2:10).

QUESTIONS AND ANSWERS:

1. **What does it mean to take up your cross and follow Jesus (Luke 14:27)?**

   - It means embracing sacrifice, obedience, and the willingness to endure hardship for Christ's sake.

2. **How does Philippians 3:7-8 describe the value of knowing Christ?**

   - Knowing Christ surpasses all earthly gains, making sacrifices worthwhile for the sake of His kingdom.

3. **What challenges can disciples expect to face (John 15:18-20)?**

   - Opposition, persecution, and rejection from the world for living a godly life.

4. **What are the rewards of faithful discipleship (Mark 10:29-30)?**

   - Spiritual blessings, eternal life, and a deeper relationship with Christ.

5. **How can believers remain faithful when discipleship feels costly?**

   - By focusing on Christ's example, relying on the Holy Spirit, and remembering the eternal rewards (2 Timothy 3:12, Revelation 2:10).

APPLICATIONS:

1. **Assess Your Commitment**: Reflect on areas where you may need to surrender more fully to Christ.

2. **Embrace Sacrifice**: Identify one way you can deny yourself to follow Jesus more faithfully.

3. **Encourage Another Disciple**: Support and pray for someone else on their journey of discipleship.

PRAYER PROMPTS:

1. Thank Jesus for His ultimate sacrifice and the privilege of following Him.

2. Pray for strength and perseverance in the face of challenges.

3. Ask for courage to fully embrace the cost of discipleship.

Glossary

As with any field of study, there are terms that are specific to that area, and a study of God's Word is no different. I have tried to define what those terms mean when used in a study so that anyone using these guides will have a "common" understanding of how I use them.

Core Doctrinal Terms

- **Justification**

  God's legal declaration that a sinner is righteous by faith in Christ, based on Christ's righteousness, not their own (Romans 5:1).

- **Sanctification**

  The lifelong process by which God makes believers holy, conforming them to the image of Christ (1 Thessalonians 4:3).

- **Glorification**

  The final state of salvation when believers are made perfect and receive resurrection bodies (Romans 8:30).

- **Redemption**

  The act of Christ purchasing sinners from the bondage of sin and death through His blood (Ephesians 1:7).

- **Salvation**

  Deliverance from sin and its consequences, granted by God through faith in Jesus Christ (Ephesians 2:8–9).

- **Election**

  God's sovereign choice, before the foundation of the world, to save certain individuals by grace (Ephesians 1:4–5).

- **Predestination**

  God's predetermined plan to bring His elect to salvation and conform them to Christ (Romans 8:29–30).

- **Atonement**

  Christ's sacrificial death on the cross that satisfies God's justice and makes reconciliation with God possible (Isaiah 53:5).

- **Propitiation**

  The appeasement of God's wrath by the sacrifice of Christ, making God favorable toward the believer (1 John 2:2).

- **Righteousness**

  The moral perfection required by God, fulfilled in Christ and credited to believers by faith (2 Corinthians 5:21).

- **Grace**

  God's unearned favor and kindness toward sinners, giving them salvation blessings they do not deserve (Titus 2:11).

- **Mercy**

  God's compassionate withholding of the judgment and punishment deserved for sin (Ephesians 2:4–5).

- **Faith**

  Trust and confidence in God, especially in His promises and in the person and work of Jesus Christ (Hebrews 11:1).

- **Works**

  Actions done in obedience to God's commands; they do not save but are evidence of true faith (James 2:17).

- **Imputation**

  The act of God crediting Christ's righteousness to believers and their sin to Christ (Romans 4:22–24).

- **Original Sin**

  The inherited sin nature and guilt from Adam's fall that affects all humanity (Romans 5:12).

- **Sin Nature**

  The inner inclination of humans to rebel against God, inherited from (Galatians 5:17).

- **Repentance**

  A sincere turning from sin to God, involving sorrow for sin and a changed heart and life (Acts 3:19).

- **Confession**

  Acknowledging one's sin before God in truth, often accompanied by repentance and faith (1 John 1:9).

- **Regeneration**

  The spiritual rebirth by which the Holy Spirit gives new life to the believer (Titus 3:5).

- **New Birth**

  Another term for regeneration; being "born again" by the Spirit through faith in Christ (John 3:3).

- **Covenant (Old Covenant / New Covenant)**

  A binding agreement made by God with His people:

  Old Covenant: The Mosaic Law given to Israel (Exodus 19–24).

  New Covenant: The promise of salvation and transformed hearts through Christ's blood (Jeremiah 31:31–34; Luke 22:20).

Christological Terms

- **Messiah**

  The Anointed One promised in the Old Testament, fulfilled in Jesus Christ, who came to save and reign as King (Daniel 9:25–26; John 4:25–26).

- **Son of God**

  A title expressing Jesus' divine nature, uniquely begotten of the Father, equal with God (John 5:18; Hebrews 1:3).

- **Son of Man**

  A title Jesus used for Himself, highlighting both His humanity and His identity as the exalted figure in Daniel's vision (Daniel 7:13–14; Mark 10:45).

- **Christ**

  The Greek equivalent of "Messiah," meaning "Anointed One," referring to Jesus as the divinely appointed Savior and King (Matthew 16:16).

- **Lamb of God**

  A title for Jesus pointing to His role as the perfect sacrificial offering who takes away the sin of the world (John 1:29).

- **Lion of Judah**

  A title for Jesus symbolizing His authority, kingship, and power, rooted in the tribe of Judah (Revelation 5:5).

- **Incarnation**

  The act of God the Son taking on human flesh in the person of Jesus Christ (John 1:14; Philippians 2:6–7).

- **Resurrection**

  The bodily rising of Jesus from the dead on the third day, proving His victory over sin and death (1 Corinthians 15:3–4).

- **Ascension**

  Jesus' return to heaven in His glorified body, where He now reigns at the right hand of the Father (Acts 1:9–11; Ephesians 1:20).

- **Mediator**

  Jesus is the one who reconciles God and humanity by His death and intercession (1 Timothy 2:5).

- **Intercessor**

  Jesus continually pleads on behalf of believers before the Father, securing their standing and help (Romans 8:34; Hebrews 7:25).

- **High Priest**

  Jesus, who offers Himself as the perfect sacrifice and continually represents believers before God (Hebrews 4:14–16).

- **Lordship of Christ**

  The truth that Jesus is sovereign over all creation and should be obeyed and worshiped as Lord (Philippians 2:9–11; Romans 10:9).

- **Deity of Christ**

  The doctrine that Jesus is fully God, possessing all the attributes of divinity (Colossians 2:9; John 1:1).

- **Jesus Christ**

  The full name of the Savior: *Jesus* (His human name, meaning "Yahweh saves") and *Christ* (His title as the Anointed One) - fully God, fully man, Redeemer and Lord (Matthew 1:21; John 20:31).

Pneumatology (Holy Spirit)

- **Holy Spirit**

  The third Person of the Trinity, fully God, who regenerates, indwells, empowers, teaches, and guides believers (John 14:26; Acts 5:3–4).

- **Indwelling**

  The permanent presence of the Holy Spirit within every true believer, beginning at salvation (Romans 8:9; 1 Corinthians 3:16).

- **Sealing**

  The Holy Spirit's mark of ownership and guarantee of the believer's eternal inheritance in Christ (Ephesians 1:13–14).

- **Spiritual Gifts**

  Special abilities given by the Holy Spirit to believers for the building up of the Church and service to others (1 Corinthians 12:4–7; Romans 12:6–8).

- **Fruit of the Spirit**

  The character traits produced in a believer's life as they walk in the Spirit (Galatians 5:22–23).

- **Conviction**

  The Holy Spirit's work of making a person aware of sin, righteousness, and judgment, leading to repentance (John 16:8).

- **Empowerment**

  The Holy Spirit's enabling of believers to live godly lives and serve effectively in ministry and witness (Acts 1:8; Galatians 5:16).

- **Anointing**

  The setting apart and empowering by the Holy Spirit for a specific purpose or ministry, often associated with teaching, leadership, or service (1 John 2:20, 27; Luke 4:18).

Anthropology (Humanity)

- **Image of God (Imago Dei)**

  The unique way human beings reflect God's nature, including rationality, morality, creativity, relationship, and dominion - giving every person inherent value (Genesis 1:26–27).

- **Total Depravity**

  The condition of humanity after the Fall, meaning every part of the human being is affected by sin, rendering people unable to seek God without divine grace (Romans 3:10–12; Ephesians 2:1).

- **Free Will**

  The capacity to choose; though human will is real, it is limited and influenced by sin until freed by God's grace (Joshua 24:15; Romans 6:17–18).

- **Body/Soul/Spirit**

  The tripartite nature of humanity:

  Body – physical aspect,

  Soul – the seat of emotions and mind,

  Spirit – the part capable of communion with God (1 Thessalonians 5:23; Hebrews 4:12).

- **Gender**

  God's intentional creation of humanity as male and female, equal in value but distinct in role and design (Genesis 1:27; Matthew 19:4–5).

- **Identity**

  A person's true self as defined by God, not by the world - for believers, it is rooted in being a new creation in Christ (2 Corinthians 5:17; Galatians 2:20).

- **Conscience**

  The inner moral compass given by God that distinguishes right from wrong, though it can be weakened or seared by sin (Romans 2:14–15; 1 Timothy 4:2).

- **Flesh vs. Spirit**

  The ongoing conflict between the sinful human nature ("flesh") and the Holy Spirit within the believer (Galatians 5:16–17; Romans 8:5–8).

- **Human Dignity**

  The inherent worth of every human life as made in God's image, regardless of age, ability, or status (Psalm 8:4–5; James 3:9).

- **Temptation**

  An enticement to sin that appeals to desire; not sin itself, but a test of obedience (James 1:13–15; Matthew 4:1–11).

- **Desire**

  God-given longings that can be holy or sinful depending on their object and direction (Psalm 37:4; James 4:1–3).

- **Self-Denial**

  The deliberate choice to forsake selfish desires and submit to God's will, essential to true discipleship (Luke 9:23; Titus 2:11–12).

Ecclesiology (Church Life)

- **Saints**

  All true believers in Christ who are set apart (sanctified) by God and called to live holy lives (Romans 1:7; 1 Corinthians 1:2).

- **Church**

  The collective body of believers in Jesus Christ, both universal (all Christians) and local (individual congregations), called out to worship, serve, and proclaim the gospel (Matthew 16:18; Acts 2:42).

- **Body of Christ**

  A metaphor describing the Church as a living organism, with Christ as the head and believers as individual members, each with unique roles (1 Corinthians 12:12–27; Ephesians 1:22–23).

- **Unity**

  The spiritual oneness of believers, founded on shared faith in Christ and maintained through love, humility, and truth (Ephesians 4:3–6; John 17:21).

- **Elders**

  Spiritually mature men appointed to lead, teach, shepherd, and oversee the church (also called pastors or overseers) (1 Timothy 3:1–7; Titus 1:5–9).

- **Discipline**

  The loving correction of sin within the Church to restore the believer and protect the holiness of the body (Matthew 18:15–17; Hebrews 12:11).

- **Fellowship**

  The deep spiritual bond among believers marked by shared life, worship, encouragement, and mutual support (Acts 2:42; 1 John 1:7).

- **Membership**

  Formal identification and commitment to a local body of believers for accountability, service, and mutual edification (Romans 12:4–5; Hebrews 13:17).

- **Priesthood of Believers**

  The truth that all Christians have direct access to God through Christ and are called to minister, pray, and serve as His representatives (1 Peter 2:5, 9; Revelation 1:6).

- **Corporate Worship**

  The gathered expression of adoration, praise, prayer, and Word-centered teaching among believers, glorifying God together (Psalm 95:6; Colossians 3:16).

- **Spiritual Authority**

  God-given leadership and oversight within the Church, exercised by pastors/elders in accordance with Scripture and under Christ's lordship (Hebrews 13:17; 1 Peter 5:2–3).

- **Church Leadership**

  Biblical leadership within the church, primarily including elders and deacons, charged with shepherding, teaching, decision-making, and modeling godly character (1 Timothy 3:1–13; Acts 20:28).

Missiology & Evangelism

- **Great Commission**

  Jesus' command to His followers to go and make disciples of all nations, baptizing them and teaching them to obey all He has commanded (Matthew 28:18–20).

- **Gospel**

  The "good news" of Jesus Christ's life, death, and resurrection to save sinners, offering forgiveness and eternal life by grace through faith (1 Corinthians 15:1–4; Romans 1:16).

- **Witness**

  A believer who testifies to the truth of Christ by words and actions, declaring what God has done in their life (Acts 1:8).

- **Evangelism**

  The act of proclaiming the gospel to others with the goal of leading them to faith in Christ (Romans 10:14–15; 2 Timothy 4:5).

- **Mission**

  The Church's God-given task to reach the world with the gospel, making Christ known among all people (John 20:21; Acts 13:47).

- **Conversion**

  The turning from sin to God in repentance and faith, resulting in a new life in Christ (Acts 3:19; 2 Corinthians 5:17).

- **Baptism**

  A public declaration of faith in Christ, symbolizing a believer's identification with Jesus' death, burial, and resurrection (Romans 6:3–4; Matthew 28:19).

- **Discipleship**

  The lifelong process of growing in Christ through obedience, learning, and following His example, often in relationship with other believers (Luke 9:23; 2 Timothy 2:2).

- **Unreached**

  People or groups who have little or no access to the gospel and no indigenous Christian community able to evangelize them (Romans 15:20).

- **Testimony**

  A personal account of how someone came to faith in Christ and what God has done in their life (Psalm 66:16; Revelation 12:11).

Christian Living & Sanctification

- **Holiness**

  Being set apart by God and for God, marked by moral purity and a life that reflects His character (1 Peter 1:15–16; Hebrews 12:14).

- **Obedience**

  Submitting to God's Word and will, out of love and faith, as evidence of true discipleship (John 14:15; James 1:22).

- **Righteous Living**

  Living in a way that aligns with God's standards, shaped by His righteousness and empowered by His Spirit (Titus 2:11–12; 1 John 3:7).

- **Spiritual Growth**

  The ongoing process of becoming more like Christ in character and conduct through the work of the Holy Spirit (2 Peter 3:18; Ephesians 4:15).

- **Prayer**

  Communication with God through praise, confession, thanksgiving, and petition, expressing dependence and relationship (Philippians 4:6; 1 Thessalonians 5:17).

- **Fasting**

  Voluntarily abstaining from food or other comforts for a time of focused prayer, repentance, or spiritual breakthrough (Matthew 6:16–18; Isaiah 58:6).

- **Worship**

  Reverent love and adoration for God expressed through praise, obedience, and devotion, both personally and corporately (John 4:24; Psalm 95:6).

- **Perseverance**

  Steadfastness in faith through trials, trusting God to sustain and complete His work in us (James 1:12; Hebrews 10:36).

- **Self-Control**

  A fruit of the Spirit involving discipline over one's thoughts, emotions, and actions to honor God (Galatians 5:23; 1 Corinthians 9:25–27).

- **Forgiveness**

  Releasing others from the debt of their wrongs as God has forgiven us in Christ, restoring relationship and peace (Ephesians 4:32; Colossians 3:13).

- **Bitterness**

  A deep-seated resentment that corrupts the soul and relationships, warned against in Scripture as spiritually dangerous (Hebrews 12:15; Ephesians **4:31).**

- **Grace vs. Legalism**

  Grace: God's unearned favor and power to save and transform.

  Legalism: Relying on rule-keeping or human effort for righteousness or favor with God (Galatians 2:21; Romans 6:14).

- **Mortification of Sin**

  The Spirit-empowered process of putting sin to death in the believer's life through repentance and obedience (Romans 8:13; Colossians 3:5).

- **Fruitfulness**

  The evidence of a transformed life that produces spiritual results - such as good works, growth in character, and influence for Christ (John 15:5; Galatians 5:22–23).

- **Overcomer**

  A believer who, through faith in Christ, resists sin, endures trials, and ultimately conquers by God's power (Revelation 2:7; 1 John 5:4–5).

- **Walking in the Spirit**

  Living under the guidance and power of the Holy Spirit, resulting in godliness and victory over sin (Galatians 5:16; Romans 8:4).

- **Bearing the Cross**

  Daily choosing to follow Jesus with self-denial and sacrifice, even when it involves suffering for His sake (Luke 9:23; Galatians 2:20).

Ethics & Apologetics

- **Truth**

  That which is consistent with the nature and Word of God; Jesus is the embodiment of truth (John 14:6; John 17:17).

- **Love**

  A selfless, sacrificial commitment to the good of others, demonstrated perfectly by God in Christ (1 Corinthians 13:4–7; 1 John 4:7–10).

- **Justice**

  God's perfect standard of fairness and righteousness, rewarding good and punishing evil without partiality (Micah 6:8; Romans 2:6–11).

- **Judgment**

  God's righteous evaluation of all people, resulting in reward for the redeemed and punishment for the wicked (Hebrews 9:27; Revelation 20:12–15).

- **Hell**

  A real, eternal place of conscious punishment and separation from God for those who reject Christ (Matthew 25:46; Revelation 20:15).

- **Heaven**

  The eternal dwelling place of God, where believers will enjoy His presence, worship, and perfect joy forever (John 14:2–3; Revelation 21:1–4).

- **Purgatory (refuted)**

  The unbiblical Roman Catholic teaching of a temporary state of purification after death. Scripture teaches that believers are immediately with the Lord upon death (2 Corinthians 5:8; Hebrews 9:27).

- **Soul Sleep (refuted)**

  The false belief that the soul becomes unconscious at death. The Bible teaches conscious existence after death (Luke 16:22–23; Philippians 1:23).

- **Annihilationism (refuted)**

  The idea that the wicked cease to exist after judgment. Scripture teaches eternal conscious punishment for the lost (Matthew 25:46; Revelation 14:11).

- **Blasphemy of the Holy Spirit**

  The persistent, willful rejection of the Holy Spirit's testimony about Christ, resulting in a hardened heart and unforgivable sin (Mark 3:29; Matthew 12:31–32).

- **Biblical Authority**

  The belief that the Bible is the inspired, inerrant, and sufficient Word of God, our final standard for truth and life (2 Timothy 3:16–17; Psalm 119:89).

- **Cultural Engagement**

  Faithful involvement in society guided by Scripture - speaking truth in love, advocating justice, and shining the light of Christ (Matthew 5:14–16; Jeremiah 29:7).

- **Political Disagreement**

  Differing political views among believers must be approached with humility, grace, and unity in Christ above all (Romans 14:1–12; Philippians 2:2–4).

- **Gender & Identity**

  God created humanity as male and female in His image. Identity is found in Christ, not in self-definition (Genesis 1:27; Galatians 3:28).

- **Transgenderism**

  The belief that one's gender can differ from biological sex contradicts God's design. Believers are called to love others while upholding the truth of God's created order (Deuteronomy 22:5; Romans 1:24–27).

- **Abortion**

  The intentional ending of unborn human life, which the Bible regards as the taking of innocent life. Every human is made in God's image from conception (Psalm 139:13–16; Exodus 20:13).

- **Forgiveness**

  Letting go of offense and extending mercy, modeled by God through Christ and required of His followers (Matthew 6:14–15; Ephesians 4:32).

- **Speech Ethics (tongue, gossip, language)**

  Believers are called to use words to build up, speak truth, avoid gossip, and reflect Christ's holiness (James 3:5–10; Ephesians 4:29; Colossians 4:6).

- **Worldliness vs. Godliness**

  Worldliness is living by sinful, fleshly values

  Godliness is living in reverence for God, shaped by truth and holiness (1 John 2:15–17; Titus 2:11–12).

Biblical & Systematic Theology

- **Trinity**

  The one true God eternally exists as three distinct Persons - Father, Son, and Holy Spirit - who are coequal, coeternal, and consubstantial (Matthew 28:19; 2 Corinthians 13:14).

- **Scripture (Sola Scriptura)**

  The belief that Scripture alone is the supreme and final authority for faith and practice, above tradition or church teachings (2 Timothy 3:16–17; Acts 17:11).

- **Inerrancy**

  The doctrine that the Bible, in its original manuscripts, is without error in all it affirms, because it is the Word of God (Proverbs 30:5; John 17:17).

- **Biblical Inspiration**

  The supernatural work of the Holy Spirit by which God guided the human authors of Scripture so that what they wrote is the very Word of God (2 Peter 1:21; 2 Timothy 3:16).

- **Canon of Scripture**

  The recognized collection of 66 inspired books (39 Old Testament, 27 New Testament) that form the authoritative Bible (Luke 24:44; Revelation 22:18–19).

- **Hermeneutics**

  The principles and methods of interpreting Scripture faithfully and accurately, seeking the intended meaning of the biblical text (Nehemiah 8:8; 2 Timothy 2:15).

- **Typology (e.g., Passover)**

  A divinely intended pattern in the Old Testament (type) that foreshadows a New Testament fulfillment (antitype), such as the Passover lamb prefiguring Christ (Exodus 12; 1 Corinthians 5:7).

- **Eschatology**

  The study of "last things," including the return of Christ, resurrection, judgment, heaven, and hell (1 Thessalonians 4:16–17; Revelation 20–22).

- **Includes:**

  Rapture – The catching up of believers to meet Christ in the air (1 Thessalonians 4:17).

  Resurrection – The raising of all the dead, the just to life, the unjust to judgment (John 5:28–29).

  Hell – Eternal punishment and separation from God for the unrepentant (Matthew 25:46).

- **Dispensationalism**

  A theological system that sees God's plan unfolding in distinct historical eras (dispensations), often emphasizing a literal interpretation of prophecy and a future for national Israel (Ephesians 1:10; Daniel 9:24–27).

- **Covenantalism**

  A theological system viewing God's relationship with humanity primarily through covenants (e.g., Covenant of Works and Covenant of Grace), emphasizing continuity between the Old and New Testaments (Genesis 12:1–3; Hebrews 8:6–13).

- **Sovereignty of God**

  God's absolute rule and authority over all creation, events, and human decisions, working all things according to His perfect will (Isaiah 46:9–10; Romans 8:28).

Spiritual Warfare

- **Armor of God**

  The spiritual defenses God provides for believers to stand firm against Satan's attacks - including truth, righteousness, faith, salvation, God's Word, and prayer (Ephesians 6:10–18).

- **Satan**

  A fallen angel who opposes God, deceives the nations, and seeks to destroy believers; the accuser, tempter, and enemy of the soul (1 Peter 5:8; Revelation 12:9–10).

- **Temptation**

  A lure or enticement to sin, coming from the flesh, the world, or the devil. It is not sin itself but a test of obedience (James 1:13–15; 1 Corinthians 10:13).

- **Victory**

  The triumph believers have over sin, death, and Satan through the finished work of Christ and the power of the Holy Spirit (1 Corinthians 15:57; Romans 8:37).

- **Prayer & Fasting**

  Spiritual disciplines involving communion with God and the denial of physical comfort to seek God's will, power, or deliverance (Matthew 6:6, 16–18; Acts 13:2–3).

- **Spiritual Discernment**

  The Spirit-enabled ability to distinguish between truth and error, right and wrong, or spirits that are from God or not (1 John 4:1; Hebrews 5:14).

- **Strongholds**

  Deep-seated patterns of sin, lies, or demonic influence that hold people in bondage, which must be torn down by truth and divine power (2 Corinthians 10:3–5).

- **Deliverance**

  The act of being set free from spiritual bondage, demonic influence, or oppression through the authority and power of Jesus Christ (Luke 4:18; Mark 1:34).

Appendix

How Do I Become a Christian, or Convert to Christianity?

These studies are designed to deepen your understanding of God's truth, strengthen your faith, and equip you to live boldly and wisely in a world of confusion and compromise. They are rooted in the conviction that **God's Word is sufficient, clear, authoritative, and necessary** for every area of life. For the believer, studying Scripture is not optional—it is essential. The Bible is how we know God, grow in holiness, discern truth from error, and walk in obedience. It renews the mind (Romans 12:2), anchors the soul (Hebrews 6:19), and equips us for every good work (2 Timothy 3:16–17). In a time when many are tossed by emotion, culture, and deception, these studies invite you to build your life on the unshakable foundation of God's Word and to grow in love, truth, and discernment as a faithful disciple of Jesus Christ.

If you are not a Christian then these studies may not make sense to you but more importantly than understanding them is your eternal destination. As a non-believer God does not permit you entrance into His Heaven but as a believer He does and openly welcomes you in. The below is a guide as to how to become a Christian, or convert to Christianity.

(This is taken from one of the topics in this series.)

Focus: Understanding what the Bible says about salvation, repentance, and faith in Christ as the only way to become a true follower of Jesus.

PRIMARY SCRIPTURE:

- John 3:16

ADDITIONAL SCRIPTURE:

- Romans 10:9–13; Acts 2:37–39; Ephesians 2:8–9; John 1:12; Luke 9:23; 2 Corinthians 5:17

Biblical Teaching

- Becoming a Christian is not about joining a religion, trying harder, or cleaning up your life—it's about being **born again** by trusting in Jesus Christ (John 3:3–7).
- You become a Christian by **repenting of your sin** and placing your **faith in Jesus** as Savior and Lord (Acts 2:38; Romans 10:9).
- Salvation is a **free gift of grace**—you cannot earn it. It is received by believing in Jesus, who died for your sins and rose again (Ephesians 2:8–9).
- True conversion includes a change of heart, a new relationship with God, and a new identity as a child of God (2 Corinthians 5:17; John 1:12).
- Following Jesus also means surrender—He calls you to deny yourself, take up your cross, and follow Him (Luke 9:23).
- After trusting in Christ, a believer should **be baptized** as a public declaration of faith and obedience (Acts 2:38).
- Every new believer is also called to **join a Christ-centered, Bible-teaching local church** where they can grow in truth, worship, and fellowship (Acts 2:42–47; Hebrews 10:24–25).

Steps from Scripture to Become a Christian

- **Admit you are a sinner** in need of salvation.
- "For all have sinned and fall short of the glory of God." (Romans 3:23)
- **Believe in Jesus Christ** as God's Son, who died for your sins and rose again.
- "Believe in the Lord Jesus, and you will be saved." (Acts 16:31)
- **Confess Jesus as Lord** and call on Him to save you.

- "If you confess with your mouth... and believe in your heart... you will be saved." (Romans 10:9)
- **Repent**—turn away from sin and turn to God.
- "Repent, and be baptized... for the forgiveness of your sins." (Acts 2:38)
- **Be baptized** as a public step of obedience and testimony to your new life.
- "Whoever believes and is baptized will be saved." (Mark 16:16)
- **Join a faithful church** that teaches God's Word and walks in the truth.
- "They devoted themselves to the apostles' teaching and to fellowship..." (Acts 2:42)

QUESTIONS AND ANSWERS

1. **What must I do to be saved?**

   - Repent of your sin and place your faith in Jesus Christ alone for salvation (Romans 10:9–13; Acts 2:38).

2. **Do I need to be baptized to become a Christian?**

   - Baptism does not save, but it is the **first step of obedience** for those who are saved—a public confession of faith (Acts 10:47–48).

3. **Is there a prayer I must pray?**

   - Scripture does not prescribe a specific prayer, but God hears a sincere cry for mercy and faith (Luke 18:13–14). Speak honestly to God and trust Him to save you.

4. **What happens after I become a Christian?**

   - You begin a new life—growing in faith, reading the Bible, praying, **getting baptized**, joining a church, and following Jesus daily (2 Corinthians 5:17; Colossians 2:6–7).

APPLICATIONS

1. If you have not yet trusted in Christ, do so today—turn from sin and receive His gift of salvation.
2. Obey Jesus by being baptized and connecting with a local, Bible-teaching church.
3. If you are a believer, help others understand the true gospel and how to respond to it.
4. Rejoice in your salvation and share your testimony with others who need Christ.

PRAYER PROMPTS

1. If you're ready to become a Christian, pray something like: "Lord Jesus, I know I am a sinner. I believe You died for my sins and rose again. I turn from my sin and trust in You as my Savior and Lord. Please forgive me, change me, and help me follow You. Amen."
2. Thank God for saving you and giving you new life through faith in Christ.
3. Pray for strength to walk in obedience, be baptized, and connect with other believers in a local church.
4. Intercede for friends and family who do not yet know Jesus, that they would come to saving faith.

Word Index

1:57 The Joy of the Lord
1:59 Living as Salt and Light
1:60 The Victory of the Cross
1:61 The Return of Christ
1:62 God's Unchanging Character
1:63 God's Love for the World

CHRISTIAN

1:20 Christian Community
1:23 The Power of Forgiveness
1:24 Living a Life of Gratitude
1:26 The Second Coming of Christ
1:61 The Return of Christ

CHURCH

1:10 The Mission of the Church
1:15 Church Discipline
1:17 The Role of Prayer in the Believer's Life
1:18 The Fruit of the Spirit and Spiritual Growth
1:19 Faith and Works
1:20 Christian Community
1:22 Spiritual Gifts
1:25 Evangelism
1:30 The Trinity
1:35 Faithfulness in Service
1:38 The Role of Worship
1:45 Biblical Leadership
1:52 The Body of Christ

COMING

1:26 The Second Coming of Christ
1:28 Judgment
1:61 The Return of Christ
1:62 God's Unchanging Character

ETERNITY

EVANGELISM

FAITH

FEAR

1:6 Stewardship and Generosity
1:16 Personal Responsibility with Regards to Salvation
1:25 Evangelism
1:40 Humility
1:42 The Fear of the Lord
1:53 The Call to Mission
1:55 The Peace of God
1:56 Christian Contentment
1:60 The Victory of the Cross

FORGIVEN

1:23 The Power of Forgiveness

FRUIT

1:5 Walking in the Spirit
1:18 The Fruit of the Spirit and Spiritual Growth
1:19 Faith and Works
1:29 Sanctification
1:32 Overcoming Sin
1:41 The Fruit of the Spirit in Action
1:47 Spiritual Maturity
1:57 The Joy of the Lord

GIFTS

1:10 The Mission of the Church
1:22 Spiritual Gifts
1:52 The Body of Christ

GOD

1:1 The Word of God
1:2 Our Identity in Christ
1:3 The Holiness of God
1:4 The Cost of Discipleship
1:5 Walking in the Spirit

1:6 Stewardship and Generosity
1:7 Rest and Sabbath
1:8 Suffering and Sovereignty
1:9 Spiritual Warfare
1:10 The Mission of the Church
1:11 Eternal Perspective
1:12 Soul Annihilation vs. Soul Eternity
1:13 Double Predestination and Its Refutation
1:14 The Reality of Hell
1:15 Church Discipline
1:16 Personal Responsibility with Regards to Salvation
1:17 The Role of Prayer in the Believer's Life
1:18 The Fruit of the Spirit and Spiritual Growth
1:19 Faith and Works
1:20 Christian Community
1:21 Perseverance in Trials
1:22 Spiritual Gifts
1:23 The Power of Forgiveness
1:24 Living a Life of Gratitude
1:25 Evangelism
1:26 The Second Coming of Christ
1:27 Heaven
1:28 Judgment
1:29 Sanctification
1:30 The Trinity
1:31 The Beatitudes
1:32 Overcoming Sin
1:33 Hope in Hardship
1:34 God's Providence
1:35 Faithfulness in Service
1:36 Wisdom in Decision-Making
1:37 God's Faithfulness
1:38 The Role of Worship
1:39 The Armor of God
1:40 Humility
1:41 The Fruit of the Spirit in Action
1:42 The Fear of the Lord
1:43 God's Justice and Mercy
1:44 The Sovereignty of God
1:45 Biblical Leadership

GOSPEL

GRACE

HARDSHIP

HELL

HOLINESS

LOVE

MERCY

MISSION

PERSEVERANCE

PRAYER

1:17 The Role of Prayer in the Believer's Life
1:18 The Fruit of the Spirit and Spiritual Growth
1:19 Faith and Works
1:20 Christian Community
1:21 Perseverance in Trials
1:22 Spiritual Gifts
1:23 The Power of Forgiveness
1:24 Living a Life of Gratitude
1:25 Evangelism
1:26 The Second Coming of Christ
1:27 Heaven
1:28 Judgment
1:29 Sanctification
1:30 The Trinity
1:31 The Beatitudes
1:32 Overcoming Sin
1:33 Hope in Hardship
1:34 God's Providence
1:35 Faithfulness in Service
1:36 Wisdom in Decision-Making
1:37 God's Faithfulness
1:38 The Role of Worship
1:39 The Armor of God
1:40 Humility
1:41 The Fruit of the Spirit in Action
1:42 The Fear of the Lord
1:43 God's Justice and Mercy
1:44 The Sovereignty of God
1:45 Biblical Leadership
1:46 Faith in God's Timing
1:47 Spiritual Maturity
1:48 God's Covenant Promises
1:49 The Power of the Gospel
1:50 The Role of Grace
1:51 The Pursuit of Holiness
1:52 The Body of Christ
1:53 The Call to Mission
1:54 The Promises of Heaven
1:55 The Peace of God
1:56 Christian Contentment

SANCTIFICATION

SECOND

STEWARDSHIP

TRIALS

TRINITY

VICTORY

WARFARE

WOMEN

Reference Index

Deuteronomy 10
>1:42 The Fear of the Lord

Joshua 1
>1:1 The Word of God

Joshua 21
>1:37 God's Faithfulness

2 Samuel 7
>1:48 God's Covenant Promises

Nehemiah 8
>1:57 The Joy of the Lord

Job 1
>1:8 Suffering and Sovereignty

Job 42
>1:44 The Sovereignty of God

Psalms 1
>1:1 The Word of God

Psalms 16
>1:57 The Joy of the Lord

Psalms 23
>1:7 Rest and Sabbath
>1:56 Christian Contentment

Psalms 24
>1:6 Stewardship and Generosity
>1:37 God's Faithfulness

Psalms 27
>1:46 Faith in God's Timing

Psalms 29
>1:38 The Role of Worship

Psalms 32
1:36 Wisdom in Decision-Making

Psalms 33
1:42 The Fear of the Lord

Psalms 34
1:31 The Beatitudes
1:33 Hope in Hardship

Psalms 37
1:31 The Beatitudes

Psalms 46
1:55 The Peace of God

Psalms 89
1:37 God's Faithfulness
1:43 God's Justice and Mercy

Psalms 91
1:39 The Armor of God

Psalms 95
1:38 The Role of Worship

Psalms 100
1:24 Living a Life of Gratitude
1:38 The Role of Worship

Psalms 102
1:62 God's Unchanging Character

Psalms 103
1:23 The Power of Forgiveness
1:63 God's Love for the World

Psalms 115
1:44 The Sovereignty of God

Psalms 119
 1:1 The Word of God
 1:9 Spiritual Warfare
 1:32 Overcoming Sin
 1:36 Wisdom in Decision-Making
 1:39 The Armor of God

Psalms 139
 1:18 The Fruit of the Spirit and Spiritual Growth
 1:34 God's Providence

Proverbs 1
 1:42 The Fear of the Lord

Proverbs 3
 1:6 Stewardship and Generosity
 1:34 God's Providence
 1:36 Wisdom in Decision-Making

Proverbs 4
 1:59 Living as Salt and Light

Proverbs 9
 1:42 The Fear of the Lord

Proverbs 15
 1:36 Wisdom in Decision-Making

Proverbs 16
 1:34 God's Providence
 1:44 The Sovereignty of God

Proverbs 19
 1:6 Stewardship and Generosity
 1:44 The Sovereignty of God

Proverbs 22
 1:40 Humility

Proverbs 27
> 1:20 Christian Community

Proverbs 28
> 1:32 Overcoming Sin

Proverbs 30
> 1:56 Christian Contentment

Ecclesiastes 3
> 1:46 Faith in God's Timing

Ecclesiastes 12
> 1:28 Judgment
> 1:36 Wisdom in Decision-Making
> 1:42 The Fear of the Lord

Isaiah 6
> 1:3 The Holiness of God
> 1:42 The Fear of the Lord
> 1:53 The Call to Mission

Isaiah 26
> 1:44 The Sovereignty of God
> 1:55 The Peace of God

Isaiah 30
> 1:36 Wisdom in Decision-Making
> 1:43 God's Justice and Mercy

Isaiah 40
> 1:21 Perseverance in Trials
> 1:33 Hope in Hardship
> 1:46 Faith in God's Timing
> 1:62 God's Unchanging Character

Isaiah 46
> 1:8 Suffering and Sovereignty
> 1:34 God's Providence
> 1:44 The Sovereignty of God

Habakkuk 3
>1:24 Living a Life of Gratitude

Malachi 3
>1:6 Stewardship and Generosity
>1:62 God's Unchanging Character

Matthew 4
>1:9 Spiritual Warfare
>1:32 Overcoming Sin
>1:39 The Armor of God

Matthew 5
>1:2 Our Identity in Christ
>1:19 Faith and Works
>1:23 The Power of Forgiveness
>1:31 The Beatitudes
>1:43 God's Justice and Mercy
>1:50 The Role of Grace
>1:51 The Pursuit of Holiness
>1:55 The Peace of God
>1:59 Living as Salt and Light

Matthew 6
>1:11 Eternal Perspective
>1:17 The Role of Prayer in the Believer's Life
>1:23 The Power of Forgiveness
>1:27 Heaven
>1:28 Judgment
>1:34 God's Providence
>1:36 Wisdom in Decision-Making
>1:54 The Promises of Heaven
>1:56 Christian Contentment

Matthew 7
>1:18 The Fruit of the Spirit and Spiritual Growth
>1:19 Faith and Works
>1:41 The Fruit of the Spirit in Action
>1:58 The Power of Prayer

Matthew 10
1:4 The Cost of Discipleship
1:42 The Fear of the Lord

Matthew 11
1:4 The Cost of Discipleship
1:7 Rest and Sabbath
1:21 Perseverance in Trials
1:31 The Beatitudes
1:55 The Peace of God

Matthew 16
1:4 The Cost of Discipleship

Matthew 18
1:15 Church Discipline
1:23 The Power of Forgiveness

Matthew 22
1:63 God's Love for the World

Matthew 23
1:40 Humility

Matthew 24
1:26 The Second Coming of Christ
1:61 The Return of Christ

Matthew 25
1:6 Stewardship and Generosity
1:14 The Reality of Hell
1:28 Judgment
1:35 Faithfulness in Service
1:61 The Return of Christ

Matthew 28
1:10 The Mission of the Church
1:25 Evangelism
1:53 The Call to Mission

Mark 2
>1:7 Rest and Sabbath

Mark 6
>1:7 Rest and Sabbath

Mark 9
>1:14 The Reality of Hell

Mark 10
>1:4 The Cost of Discipleship

Mark 11
>1:17 The Role of Prayer in the Believer's Life
>1:58 The Power of Prayer

Mark 16
>1:25 Evangelism

Luke 6
>1:31 The Beatitudes

Luke 9
>1:4 The Cost of Discipleship

Luke 12
>1:56 Christian Contentment

Luke 13
>1:16 Personal Responsibility with Regards to Salvation

Luke 14
>1:4 The Cost of Discipleship

Luke 16
>1:14 The Reality of Hell

Luke 17
>1:24 Living a Life of Gratitude

1:54 The Promises of Heaven
1:55 The Peace of God

John 15

1:4 The Cost of Discipleship
1:18 The Fruit of the Spirit and Spiritual Growth
1:19 Faith and Works
1:31 The Beatitudes
1:32 Overcoming Sin
1:41 The Fruit of the Spirit in Action
1:57 The Joy of the Lord

John 16

1:5 Walking in the Spirit
1:25 Evangelism

John 19

1:60 The Victory of the Cross

John 20

1:10 The Mission of the Church
1:53 The Call to Mission

Acts 1

1:5 Walking in the Spirit
1:10 The Mission of the Church
1:25 Evangelism
1:26 The Second Coming of Christ
1:53 The Call to Mission
1:61 The Return of Christ

Acts 2

1:16 Personal Responsibility with Regards to Salvation
1:20 Christian Community
1:52 The Body of Christ

Acts 4

1:49 The Power of the Gospel

Acts 20

1:6 Stewardship and Generosity

Romans 1
1:25 Evangelism
1:49 The Power of the Gospel

Romans 2
1:28 Judgment

Romans 3
1:19 Faith and Works
1:43 God's Justice and Mercy

Romans 5
1:2 Our Identity in Christ
1:21 Perseverance in Trials
1:29 Sanctification
1:50 The Role of Grace
1:55 The Peace of God
1:63 God's Love for the World

Romans 6
1:3 The Holiness of God
1:14 The Reality of Hell
1:29 Sanctification
1:32 Overcoming Sin
1:50 The Role of Grace

Romans 8
1:2 Our Identity in Christ
1:5 Walking in the Spirit
1:8 Suffering and Sovereignty
1:11 Eternal Perspective
1:17 The Role of Prayer in the Believer's Life
1:18 The Fruit of the Spirit and Spiritual Growth
1:21 Perseverance in Trials
1:24 Living a Life of Gratitude
1:32 Overcoming Sin
1:33 Hope in Hardship
1:34 God's Providence

1 Corinthians 5
>1:15 Church Discipline

1 Corinthians 10
>1:32 Overcoming Sin

1 Corinthians 12
>1:20 Christian Community
>1:52 The Body of Christ

1 Corinthians 15
>1:35 Faithfulness in Service
>1:49 The Power of the Gospel
>1:60 The Victory of the Cross

2 Corinthians 1
>1:8 Suffering and Sovereignty
>1:21 Perseverance in Trials

2 Corinthians 3
>1:5 Walking in the Spirit
>1:29 Sanctification
>1:51 The Pursuit of Holiness

2 Corinthians 4
>1:8 Suffering and Sovereignty
>1:11 Eternal Perspective
>1:21 Perseverance in Trials
>1:26 The Second Coming of Christ
>1:33 Hope in Hardship
>1:54 The Promises of Heaven

2 Corinthians 5
>1:2 Our Identity in Christ
>1:10 The Mission of the Church
>1:16 Personal Responsibility with Regards to Salvation
>1:23 The Power of Forgiveness
>1:25 Evangelism
>1:27 Heaven
>1:28 Judgment

Ephesians 1
1:2 Our Identity in Christ
1:44 The Sovereignty of God

Ephesians 2
1:16 Personal Responsibility with Regards to Salvation
1:19 Faith and Works
1:49 The Power of the Gospel
1:50 The Role of Grace
1:63 God's Love for the World

Ephesians 3
1:63 God's Love for the World

Ephesians 4
1:10 The Mission of the Church
1:20 Christian Community
1:23 The Power of Forgiveness
1:41 The Fruit of the Spirit in Action
1:47 Spiritual Maturity
1:52 The Body of Christ

Ephesians 5
1:5 Walking in the Spirit
1:24 Living a Life of Gratitude
1:59 Living as Salt and Light

Ephesians 6
1:9 Spiritual Warfare
1:17 The Role of Prayer in the Believer's Life
1:39 The Armor of God
1:58 The Power of Prayer

Philippians 1
1:18 The Fruit of the Spirit and Spiritual Growth
1:29 Sanctification
1:34 God's Providence
1:41 The Fruit of the Spirit in Action

Philippians 2

1:16 Personal Responsibility with Regards to Salvation
1:19 Faith and Works
1:29 Sanctification
1:35 Faithfulness in Service
1:40 Humility
1:44 The Sovereignty of God
1:59 Living as Salt and Light

Philippians 3
1:4 The Cost of Discipleship
1:11 Eternal Perspective
1:27 Heaven
1:47 Spiritual Maturity
1:54 The Promises of Heaven

Philippians 4
1:6 Stewardship and Generosity
1:9 Spiritual Warfare
1:17 The Role of Prayer in the Believer's Life
1:24 Living a Life of Gratitude
1:34 God's Providence
1:36 Wisdom in Decision-Making
1:55 The Peace of God
1:56 Christian Contentment
1:57 The Joy of the Lord
1:58 The Power of Prayer

Colossians 1
1:18 The Fruit of the Spirit and Spiritual Growth
1:47 Spiritual Maturity
1:49 The Power of the Gospel
1:52 The Body of Christ

Colossians 2
1:9 Spiritual Warfare
1:60 The Victory of the Cross

Colossians 3
1:2 Our Identity in Christ
1:3 The Holiness of God

2 Thessalonians 3
> 1:15 Church Discipline

1 Timothy 6
> 1:6 Stewardship and Generosity
> 1:56 Christian Contentment

2 Timothy 1
> 1:5 Walking in the Spirit
> 1:25 Evangelism

2 Timothy 2
> 1:16 Personal Responsibility with Regards to Salvation
> 1:37 God's Faithfulness

2 Timothy 3
> 1:1 The Word of God
> 1:4 The Cost of Discipleship
> 1:18 The Fruit of the Spirit and Spiritual Growth
> 1:31 The Beatitudes
> 1:47 Spiritual Maturity

2 Timothy 4
> 1:26 The Second Coming of Christ

Titus 2
> 1:19 Faith and Works
> 1:26 The Second Coming of Christ
> 1:50 The Role of Grace
> 1:61 The Return of Christ

Titus 3
> 1:19 Faith and Works

Hebrews 2
> 1:60 The Victory of the Cross

Hebrews 4
> 1:1 The Word of God

James 1

    1:1 The Word of God
    1:8 Suffering and Sovereignty
    1:17 The Role of Prayer in the Believer's Life
    1:21 Perseverance in Trials
    1:29 Sanctification
    1:33 Hope in Hardship
    1:36 Wisdom in Decision-Making
    1:47 Spiritual Maturity
    1:57 The Joy of the Lord
    1:62 God's Unchanging Character

James 2

    1:16 Personal Responsibility with Regards to Salvation
    1:19 Faith and Works
    1:43 God's Justice and Mercy

James 3

    1:41 The Fruit of the Spirit in Action
    1:42 The Fear of the Lord

James 4

    1:9 Spiritual Warfare
    1:39 The Armor of God
    1:40 Humility

James 5

    1:15 Church Discipline
    1:17 The Role of Prayer in the Believer's Life
    1:58 The Power of Prayer

1 Peter 1

    1:3 The Holiness of God
    1:29 Sanctification
    1:33 Hope in Hardship
    1:51 The Pursuit of Holiness

1 Peter 2

    1:2 Our Identity in Christ

1:3 The Holiness of God
1:38 The Role of Worship

Revelation 12

1:37 God's Faithfulness
1:60 The Victory of the Cross

Revelation 20

1:14 The Reality of Hell
1:28 Judgment

Revelation 21

1:8 Suffering and Sovereignty
1:11 Eternal Perspective
1:26 The Second Coming of Christ
1:27 Heaven
1:54 The Promises of Heaven

Revelation 22

1:26 The Second Coming of Christ
1:61 The Return of Christ

Category Index

=== Apologetics and False Teaching ===
1:12 Soul Annihilation vs. Soul Eternity
1:13 Double Predestination and Its Refutation

=== Church Life and Leadership ===
1:10 The Mission of the Church
1:15 Church Discipline
1:45 Biblical Leadership

=== Holy Spirit and Spiritual Gifts ===
1:5 Walking in the Spirit
1:18 The Fruit of the Spirit and Spiritual Growth
1:22 Spiritual Gifts
1:41 The Fruit of the Spirit in Action

=== Justice, Judgment, and Mercy ===
1:14 The Reality of Hell
1:28 Judgment

=== Prayer and Worship ===
1:17 The Role of Prayer in the Believer's Life
1:38 The Role of Worship
1:58 The Power of Prayer

=== Salvation and the Gospel ===
1:9 Spiritual Warfare
1:16 Personal Responsibility with Regards to Salvation
1:19 Faith and Works
1:29 Sanctification
1:40 Humility
1:42 The Fear of the Lord
1:46 Faith in God's Timing
1:47 Spiritual Maturity
1:49 The Power of the Gospel
1:50 The Role of Grace

1:51 The Pursuit of Holiness
1:53 The Call to Mission
1:54 The Promises of Heaven
1:56 Christian Contentment
1:57 The Joy of the Lord
1:59 Living as Salt and Light
1:60 The Victory of the Cross

=== Sin, Repentance, and Forgiveness ===
1:23 The Power of Forgiveness
1:32 Overcoming Sin

=== Spiritual Growth and Discipleship ===
1:4 The Cost of Discipleship

=== The Nature of God ===
1:1 The Word of God
1:3 The Holiness of God
1:34 God's Providence
1:37 God's Faithfulness
1:39 The Armor of God
1:43 God's Justice and Mercy
1:44 The Sovereignty of God
1:48 God's Covenant Promises
1:55 The Peace of God
1:62 God's Unchanging Character
1:63 God's Love for the World

=== The Person and Work of Christ ===
1:2 Our Identity in Christ
1:26 The Second Coming of Christ
1:52 The Body of Christ
1:61 The Return of Christ

=== The Trinity ===
1:30 The Trinity

=== Uncategorized ===
1:6 Stewardship and Generosity
1:7 Rest and Sabbath

www.ingramcontent.com/pod-product-compliance
Lightning Source LLC
Chambersburg PA
CBHW051140120626

46547CB00012B/882